marathon

from start to finish

marathon
from start to finish

sam murphy

First published 2004 by
A & C Black publishers Ltd
38 Soho Square, London W1D 3HB
www.acblack.com

Copyright © 2004 Sam Murphy
Reprinted 2007

ISBN 978 0 7136 6844 5

A CIP catalogue record for this book is available from the British Library.

Cover design, text design and page layout by Lilla Nwenu-Msimang
Cover image © Zefa/D. Madison
Photos on pages iii, viii, x, 3, 9, 13, 14, 17, 21, 22, 27, 29, 32, 33, 40 (bottom), 42 (top), 43, 44, 48, 56, 65, 66, 80, 83, 85, 87, 89, 101, 102, 110, 121, 123, 124, 127, 130, 137, 138, 140, 142, 146, 147, 148, 151, 152, 154, 157, 164, 168, 173 © Mike King
Photos on pages v, 10, 23, 24, 35, 38, 40 (top), 42 (bottom), 49-55, 58, 59-62, 91, 104, 133 © Grant Pritchard
Photo on page 41 © Cathrine Wessel /CORBIS
Photo on page 84 © Richard Smith /CORBIS
Photo on page 128 © Randy Faris /CORBIS
Photo on page 154 0 © Anne-Marie Weber /CORBIS
Illustrations © Louise Parker

This book is produced using paper that is made from wood grown in managed, sustainable forests. It is natural, renewable and recyclable. The logging and manufacturing processes conform to the environmental regulations of the country of origin.
Printed and bound in Singapore by Tien Wah Press Pte.

acknowledgements

A big thank you to all those people who contributed their time, expertise and insights to this marathon project!

First and foremost to John Brewer, director of the Human Performance Centre at Lilleshall National Sports Centre, for his assistance in developing this idea and for designing the training programmes; to Pauline Beare and Peg Jordan from the Women's Running Network, for feedback on various chapters; to Dr Sharon Dixon, from Exeter University, for shoe/biomechanics expertise; to Alan Watson, chartered physiotherapist and founder of the BIMAL Sports Injury Clinic in London, for advice on stretching, shoes and injury prevention; Sarah Connors, physiotherapist for UK Athletics and founder of Back on Track Sports Injury Clinic in south London, for spending time and effort helping me with the Body Maintenance section and other sections; Mike Gratton, elite marathon runner and running holiday guide; and Emma Murphy for additional research. Thanks also to Keith Anderson and Paul Magner from Trailplus for letting me gatecrash their marathon training camp with a photographer, and to all those who took part in the photographs.

My thanks also go to Charlotte Croft and Hannah McEwen for putting the book together so well, and to the photographers Mike King and Grant Pritchard. Thanks also to Ian Mitchell and the team at Pavilions in the Park, Horsham, for providing the location for our indoor photos.

Finally, a huge thank you to all the marathoners who took the time and effort to offer their feedback, tips and insights on the ultimate endurance sport. I hope you all continue to smash your PBs.

sam murphy

contents

introduction

The population is divided into those who have completed a marathon, and those who have not. Not long from now, you'll be joining the ranks of those who have. Welcome, and congratulations!

The marathon is unique among sports events. It's doubtful that you'll ever get to play against the Williams sisters at Wimbledon – your local football team isn't likely to get the chance to compete against a Premiership club, and yet you can limber up on the same start line as the marathon greats, run the same course and distance, and cross the same finish line (if a little later), that they do. That's what makes embarking on the marathon journey so magical. Like, say, climbing Mount Everest, it is many people's idea of the ultimate challenge – daunting and exciting in equal measures. Unlike conquering Everest, however, running a marathon is surprisingly achievable for the majority of people. But it takes preparation, knowledge, inspiration and dedication.

Imagine if you were to climb Everest – the preparation would start months in advance, you'd have expert assistance in planning your route, determining how far you are going to cover each day, what you are going to eat and drink, what you're going to wear, what you'll do if you encounter an injury or adverse weather. You'd study the mountain, listen to the advice and stories of others who had gone before and become familiar with the challenges, risks and pitfalls involved in your task.

Yet many of the thousands of people who embark on the ultimate running challenge each year have no idea where to begin, how much running they need to do, what they should wear, eat, drink, how and why they should warm up, stretch, cool down, take rest days... The end result is that many ditch the idea long before the big day, others drop out halfway round, and still others don't achieve the result they hoped and believed they would.

This book is designed to guide you through the whole process, so that won't happen to you! While I can't get up and train for you on those dark wintry mornings, I can certainly help you prepare in the best possible way in order to reach your goals, I can inspire and inform you, and ensure that you are as ready as you possibly can be, by the time you reach the start line. If your goal is to complete rather than compete – then you are in the right place.

And the good news is that it is perfectly possible to train for a marathon without giving up your job, your friends, your hobbies, your sex life, your Friday night out or your favourite food treats. Nor does it have to take over every waking minute. The key to success is to train, not strain. And *Marathon – from start to finish* is here to show you how – every step of the way. Whether this is your first ever marathon, or one of many, it can help make your race a success.

See you on the start line...

starting out

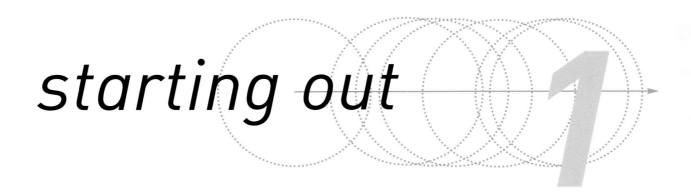

⟫ 0–26.2 miles

THE CHALLENGE OF RISING FROM THE SOFA TO COMPLETE THE MARATHON

26.2 miles, 42 km – whatever way you put it, a long way, and an immense physical and mental challenge for all those who tackle it, whether they finish in 2 1/2 or 5 1/2 hours. The physiological demands involved in running a marathon are a far cry from those of normal daily life.

Take a typical day at the office – heart rate seldom rises above 70–80 beats per minute, you only break into a sweat if the computer system crashes, and you may cover a total distance on your feet of 2–3 kilometres. Drinking is limited to a few cups of tea or coffee and the odd glass of water, and the closest you get to physical stress is having to climb the stairs if the lift isn't working. Things don't change much at home – feet up in front of the telly, remote control nearby and, at the end of a typical day, total energy expenditure of around 2,500 calories if you're a man, a tad under 2,000 if you're a woman. The same number – give or take – that you'll be burning in the course of running the marathon in a few months' time.

In the process of running 26.2 miles, you'll make approximately 40,000 strides, 20,000 with each leg – 2–3 times your bodyweight being exerted each time. If you weigh 70 kg, that's a force equal to 5.6 million kg going through your joints (it's no wonder we shrink by approximately 2 cm during the race). Your heart rate will rise to roughly 150 beats per minute, assuming you are running at around 70 per cent of your maximum aerobic capacity (the pace most non-elite marathoners instinctively choose, according to research from Loughborough University).

In a four-hour marathon, that equals a total of 36,000 beats – twice as many as normal, enabling you to pump up to 25–30 litres of blood around your body each minute. Compare this to only five litres a minute at rest and you can see that the heart needs to adapt in the same way as any other muscle to the extra demands placed upon it. Your breathing rate will also go through the roof – increasing to approximately 40 breaths a minute compared to a resting rate of between 8 and 12 breaths a minute.

It's enough to make you exhausted just thinking about it! So what changes need to take place, in order to facilitate the transformation from couch potato to accomplished endurance athlete? Broadly speaking, they can be divided into four areas:

❯ *Improved cardiovascular and respiratory fitness.* A stronger heart, lungs and circulatory system will get more oxygen and nutrients into and around the body, and dispel carbon dioxide and waste products more efficiently.

❯ *Improved fuel utilization.* The body can use carbohydrate, fat or, to a lesser extent, protein as fuel for energy production, but its preferred – and most efficient – source is carbohydrate, which it stores in the muscles and liver as a substance called glycogen. However, it can store only a limited amount – enough for perhaps two hours of exercise. Through training, you can increase your body's capacity to use fat as a fuel by as much as 30 per cent, thereby 'sparing' precious glycogen (not to mention improving health and trimming away excess pounds).

❯ *Improved muscular strength and endurance.* Strong, fatigue-resistant muscles will be able to contract for prolonged periods without tiring, and will be less susceptible to injury. They will also be able to store more glycogen – studies show increases of up to 40 per cent in trained runners – and take up more oxygen.

❯ *Stronger tendons, ligaments and bones.* Stronger connective tissues and bone will be better able to withstand the rigours of repetitive impact and reduce the risk of stress fractures and injuries to joints.

Provided you train wisely, consistently and regularly, these adaptations *will* happen, and, rest assured, you will make it to the start line – and finish line – without succumbing to injury, boredom or burnout. Read on to find out how!

Should I start training as soon as I've put in my application?

Novice runners
Begin some regular, light exercise from the day you apply and start the Body Maintenance Workout on page 56. If you can walk briskly for 30 minutes, follow the Absolute Beginners Programme on page 15.

Occasional runners (1–2 times a week)
Concentrate on building up the duration of your runs, and see the Body Maintenance Workout on pages 59–62. Concentrate on any areas that have caused you problems or injuries before, such as your back or knees. Embark on one of the training programmes 16 weeks before race day.

Regular runners (3–6 times a week)
Your constant state of training means you can afford to wait until you're certain of acceptance – then start the training programme of your choice 16 weeks before. You may want to look at the Body Maintenance Workout as your mileage increases, to prevent injuries and maintain muscular balance.

⁚ On your marks

DETERMINING YOUR STARTING POINT AND COMMITMENT

With a marathon set in your sights, you know where you are going, which is the first rule of goal setting – but do you know where you are right now?

Whether you are already a regular runner or haven't even been out to buy your running shoes yet, it's a good idea to see just how fit (or unfit!) you actually are before embarking on a training programme. This will enable you to start at a safe and effective level, rather than plunging in with both feet and ending up injured or totally disillusioned.

If you have any doubts about your ability to start running, if you have been completely sedentary for more than a year, or if you are a woman over 55 or a man over 45, it is advisable to have a check-up from your GP before you start. In addition, visit your GP if you answer 'YES' to any of the questions overleaf.

	YES	NO
Has your doctor ever said that you have a heart condition?	☐	☐
Do you feel pain in your chest when you do physical activity?	☐	☐
In the past month, have you had chest pain when you were not doing physical activity?	☐	☐
Do you lose your balance because of dizziness, or do you ever lose consciousness?	☐	☐
Do you have a bone or joint problem (such as osteoarthritis or osteoporosis) or an injury that could be made worse by physical activity?	☐	☐
Are you currently taking medication for high blood pressure or a heart condition OR is your blood pressure higher than 160/90?	☐	☐
Are you pregnant or have you recently had a baby?	☐	☐
Is your BMI (see opposite) greater than 30?	☐	☐
Do you have a parent, brother or sister who has or had premature heart disease (in men under 55 or women under 65)?	☐	☐

If you answered 'NO' to all the questions above, you get the go-ahead to start training, but do read the following advice first...

- If you are suffering from an injury, pain, infection or illness of any kind, delay starting training until it has passed or been addressed.

- If you have suffered overuse injuries in the past or have any kind of postural or biomechanical abnormalities (such as a scoliosis, fallen arches or a leg length discrepancy), it is advisable to visit a physiotherapist or podiatrist for an assessment before you begin running.

- If you are unable to walk briskly for 30 minutes comfortably, spend the next 3–4 weeks working up to this goal before moving on to the Absolute Beginner's programme on page 15.

why we are here

Running just 10 miles a week burns 1000 calories, cuts your risk of heart disease by 20%, combats depression and lowers your chances of catching a cold. Get those trainers on...

Testing times

The three tests below are designed to give a 'snapshot' of where you are now, and will help you determine what level to begin training at.

TEST 1 Resting pulse rate

Resting heart, or pulse, rate means the number of times your heat beats per minute to pump blood around the body. The average resting pulse rate is around 70 beats per minute, but don't worry if yours is different; it can vary widely. As you get fitter, more blood is forced from the heart with each beat – therefore your heart can afford to slow down, and still supply the body with the same amount of oxygen and blood. This means that resting pulse rate is a good indicator of changes in fitness.

TIP: Take your resting pulse once a week or fortnight after you've started your training, to monitor progress. Any marked increase in resting pulse rate is a possible sign of illness, infection or over-training, and a cue to take a couple of days off.

How to measure resting pulse rate

Using two fingers (not your thumb), place them on the thumb side of the underside of your wrist and locate your pulse. Count for a full minute (the first beat is '0') for accuracy. Make sure you are in a fully rested state – the ideal time is first thing in the morning before you get out of bed.

Resting pulse	Score
Below 65	3 pts
66–75	2 pts
76+	1 pt

TEST 2 Body mass index (BMI)

BMI is a measure of body weight in relation to height and is used to determine whether someone is overweight. It's not ideal, however, as it cannot distinguish between fat and muscle (so a very muscled man, like Frank Bruno, may appear to be overweight when he is not).

Simply take your weight (in kilograms) divided by height (in metres), squared. So for example, if your height is 1.70m, and your weight is 75 kg, your BMI would be:

$75/(1.7 \times 1.7) = 25.95$

The ideal range is 18.5–24.9. If your BMI is over 30, you should consider sticking to something with less impact than running, or aim to lose some weight before you begin marathon training, so as to avoid putting undue stress on your system. You may find that your BMI is below 18.5. So long as you are in good health (and, in the case of women, are menstruating normally) don't worry – it probably just means that you have the ideal physique for a marathon runner!

BMI results	Score
18.5–24.9	3 pts
25–29.9	2 pts
30+	1 pt

TEST 3 Two-mile walk/run

Using a treadmill or an outdoor route (you can measure it in your car or do eight laps plus an additional 25 metres at your local athletics track), cover a two-mile flat route as quickly as possible. You may combine walking and running or jog/run the whole route, but try not to stop at all.

Warm-up first, with some gentle mobilisations and brisk walking or marching on the spot (see page 49 for a runner's warm-up).

Compare your results with those shown below:

Men	Women	Score
Less than 15 min	Less than 16 min	6 pts
15–20 min	16–22 min	4 pts
20 min +	22 min +	2 pts

Interpreting the results

Once you've completed all three tests, add your scores together and check out the training categories below, to see which fitness level you come under. The three marathon training programmes on pages 67–79 offer two different levels of intensity, to fit in with these scores. If, however, you are a complete beginner, then turn to page 16 for your starter's orders and a simple 8-week programme to follow.

Training category	Score
Level 1	Up to 7 points
Level 2	8 points or above (max 12)

How committed are you?

What you are capable of achieving on marathon day isn't just down to your fitness level. It's also going to be influenced by how much time, effort and commitment you are able and willing to put in. It may be that you simply want to get round in one piece, and intend to put in only the bare minimum of effort – or you may be planning to go all-out and do everything you can to ensure you cross the finish line in a time you are proud of. However you feel about your marathon goal, the training programmes in this book

have been designed to accommodate you, so don't worry if you weren't planning to devote six days a week to your training. But if you can't realistically fit in even three days a week, the chances are you won't achieve the fitness level that the marathon demands. The questions below will help you think about your commitment level. Consider them carefully, and then continue for some real-life inspiration and advice on fitting marathon training into your life.

- ✥ How many days a week can I train?
- ✥ Is there a major commitment in my life between now and my marathon that may conflict (such as a wedding, house move, career challenge or visiting relative)?
- ✥ Is my finish time important to me, or do I just want to 'get round'?
- ✥ Is my lifestyle stable enough to enable me to schedule in runs?
- ✥ What does my partner/family feel about me running the marathon? (It will help if you have some support pledged for tasks that are normally your responsibility.)

why we are here

Your brain will benefit as much as your body from regular exercise. A study undertaken by the University of Illinois found that a 30-minute bout of treadmill running improved decision-making, reaction time and the number of correct answers given in a computer-based test.

⫶ Marathon training in the real world

HOW, WHERE AND WHEN TO FIT IN YOUR TRAINING

For many of us, life is a constant race against time – we juggle work, family commitments, chores and social activities, and there never seem to be enough hours in the day. So how, exactly, are you going to cram in all those hours of marathon training? You'll be glad to know that this book takes a practical stance to marathon training – the programmes are geared not only towards varying levels of experience and fitness but also to how much time you have available. You'll find full details on pages 67–79, but in the meantime let's look at some real strategies that people have used to fit training into a busy life with success.

Run to work

You get Mondays off from running because this is the day that you carry in all your work and training clothes for the week – and shower gear. The rest of the week, you run to the office and get showered and changed and take public transport home.

Advantages: It saves money and releases you from the stress of commuting. It means you use your time productively. It also doesn't impinge on family or partner time. (You may not want to run home from work if it means navigating busy streets, but if you take running gear in the car and park at the station, you can run a circular route from there.)

Disadvantages: Pollution and traffic; unpleasant surroundings (possibly); need to leave earlier to allow time to stretch, shower and change.

Lunch hour runs

These are best used for shorter, faster runs to allow you to warm-up, cool down and stretch without going over the allotted hour.

Advantages: It gives you an energy boost for the afternoon. It leaves your evenings free for other things. It gives you a mental break from work.

Disadvantages: Time is always of the essence, so even if you're feeling great you can't just keep running. Not all offices have showering facilities. You need to make time to eat. You don't get to socialise with work colleagues.

Jog a dog

Walking the dog is something you just have to do, so why not take him running with you? If your route is too long for Rover to come the whole way, circle back to the car or your house, deposit him there with a bowl of water and continue on. Alternatively, if your canine pal likes chasing a ball or Frisbee, simply throw the item and then try to race the dog to retrieve it, and repeat until one of you is exhausted. This is an informal way to introduce some speedwork.

Advantages: You get an important job done without wasting time. You get more fun from your run with a canine companion. You get a fitter dog! See pages 87–8 for tips on four-legged running companions.

Disadvantages: You can't leave the dog in the car on a hot day. Some dogs don't like to run, or aren't able to. Your run may be interrupted by the dog's antics. There's also risk of tripping or colliding into your opponent. The dog always wins!

One way ticket

Rather than doing an 'out and back' route, run from home to a local pub or café and get a friend or partner to meet you there with the car, or take a train or bus somewhere and run back.

Getting others involved

:• Get the kids to help with your fundraising activities if you are running for charity.

:• Get someone to set up a 'drinks station' for you to practise drinking on the run.

:• Don't allow running to clash with regular family or partner activities, such as Sunday lunch or Friday night cinema visits – it's the fastest way to get people to resent your running!

:• Encourage friends, kids or partners to come for a day in the country, where they can walk or bike at a leisurely pace while you run – you can then all meet up afterwards for tea and cakes!

:• Book a weekend away somewhere nice to run and take the family – even if you do two runs, that's only 2–3 hours out of the weekend 'family time'.

:• Consider taking the whole family to your marathon venue so it becomes something for them to look forward to as well as you.

Where shall I run?

There's no end of places that you can run: municipal parks, playing fields, nature trails, country parks, orienteering routes, towpaths, cycle paths, athletics tracks, beaches and public footpaths all provide great running settings. Marathon training is the perfect way for you to discover your local area, and explore a little further afield. Buy in an Ordnance Survey map so that you can see where the footpaths and greener areas are. Of course, you'll be road running too, but it's important to vary your surfaces.

Don't fear to tread

Many new runners first experience running on the treadmill. It's only when they get up to 20–30 minutes that they start wondering about running outdoors. While you may have 'graduated' to outdoor running by now, there is still a place for the treadmill in a marathon training programme, especially when it comes to timed efforts. There are also the 'safety and softy' factors to consider: it may be too dark or icy to run outdoors, or you simply may prefer to stay inside when it's wet and cold.

However, it would be foolish to do all your marathon training on the treadmill, since although the general movement pattern is the same, the biomechanics are subtly different. For a start, you aren't moving forward but running on the spot, secondly your stride length may be shortened, and thirdly, many people have a tendency to look down rather than ahead, misaligning the head and spine as they do so. And, of course, you don't have wind resistance to contend with, or any uneven surfaces.

So how can you use the treadmill to your advantage?

Make use of the incline button

Don't shy away from hills even if your intended marathon is as flat as a pancake. Hills build leg strength and boost endurance. Try some hill repeats on the treadmill with a jog recovery on the flat.

Go for speed

Whether it's a sustained 20–30 minute effort, or an interval session, you can more precisely control your speed and sustain your effort on a treadmill than out in the real world, where you may slack off without really noticing.

Do a time trial

Your ability to precisely control the environment makes the treadmill a good location for monthly time trials. Warm-up first, then select your time (12 minutes is a good test) or distance and go for it. Keep a record of your results to monitor progress.

Get feedback

Many treadmills offer feedback on heart rate, which is very useful to know. For example, you may find that running at 13 kph elevates your heart rate to 152 bpm when you first measure it, and that, weeks later, you can run 13 kph at just 147 bpm. That's progress!

Going 'off-road'

Paula Radcliffe is one of many athletes who do most of their training 'off-road'. A study found that running at the same pace on rough terrain compared to flat road burned 26 per cent more calories – so regular off-road training will make that road run feel all the easier.

It's a good idea to do at least some of your runs on soft terrain to save your joints from the constant, relentless impact of pavement or road. Not only that, but running on varied surfaces places an extra demand on the ligaments, tendons and muscles, which helps to develop strength and prevent injuries.

Much of the pleasure from running comes from its ability to provide an escape from the humdrum of daily life – and running in the fresh air, in wide open spaces and among pleasant scenery is undoubtedly more motivating than a busy cityscape. It's not so easy to measure mileage when you're off-road, but the undulating terrain and more forgiving surface make it very worthwhile, and you should get a reasonable idea by using one of the methods in the box overleaf.

If you choose to run on the beach, try to avoid highly cambered beaches, which will throw your spine and pelvis out of alignment. You'll also need to go easy on soft sand, as the 'give' of the surface enables your feet to sink and puts extra stress on your calf muscles and Achilles tendon. Trail and grass are the ideal compromise as far as the advantages and disadvantages of off-road running are concerned. Challenging, but not so much that they'll slow you down too much. Unstable, but not so much that they'll pose biomechanical problems.

Getting on track

If you live close to an athletics track, make use of it. Don't see it as an exclusive club for the elite runner, but as a convenient, flat training option, offering a forgiving surface and measurable distances. Nowadays, you are just as likely to see someone walking round the outside lane of the track as you are to see middle distance runners hurtling round the bends. It's also very handy in that you can leave a drink by the side of the track, throw off a layer of clothing once you've warmed up, or nip to the loo – all within a few metres of the clubhouse or changing rooms. Most tracks charge a small usage fee, although if you join a running club that trains at the track, this will probably be included.

Counting the miles

- Use the speedometer on a mountain bike to measure your miles.

- Wear a pedometer (a device that uses your pre-entered stride length and the number of strides you make to calculate distance covered).

- Invest in a Speed Distance Monitor – these calculate not just how far you've travelled but at what speed and km pace per hour. There are two types – global positioning systems (GPS), which rely on satellite navigation, constantly tracking your position, exact speed and distance covered – and trainer-borne velocity monitors that need to be calibrated first, and then transmit data to a wrist watch in the same manner as a heart rate monitor.

- Use a digital map reader to re-trace your route on a map. Alternatively, use a piece of string and a ruler.

- As a very broad guide, use your average mile pace plus 1 minute to estimate your 'off-road' distance. (For example, normal mile pace = 8 minutes: trail pace = 9 minutes.)

When shall I run?

Is there an ideal time to run? Yes – the ideal time to run is the time that suits you best. It may be that you love to get up and run first thing, or that you find running helps you to unwind in the evening. Fine. While research shows that between 4 and 7 pm the body is at its most receptive to training (body temperature, muscle strength and flexibility peak between these hours), it doesn't always fit in with our lifestyle. You may also have heard about a recent study that found that early morning workouts could leave your immune system compromised, and make you more susceptible to infections. It's to do with hormone levels rising and falling throughout the day, and the fact that saliva, which protects the membranes against airborne germs, is less abundant in the morning.

But don't be too quick to generalise with regard to these findings – the study was on swimmers, and their training volume was massive. Other research has shown that people who exercise in the morning are more likely to stick with an exercise programme than are those who leave it until later in the day (and are more likely to put if off altogether).

Wherever and whenever you choose to run, make a pledge right now to keep your training in perspective. There will always be times when you simply can't stick to what you had planned, and times when your body will be screaming for rest, and it is vital that you listen and pay heed to the call if you are to make it not just to the finish line, but to the start line, with a smile on your face.

Running and the menstrual cycle

A study published in the Journal of Psychosomatic Research found that three months of regular exercise successfully reduced premenstrual symptoms. But if you are already active, and can't shake PMS, it is worth considering your diet. While your metabolic rate does rise prior to your period, the extra 150–200 calories you need to meet this increased energy demand doesn't explain the cravings for sweet or carbohydrate-rich foods that many women experience. Experts believe these may be due to an increased need for magnesium. Ensure that you are getting sufficient magnesium in your diet. The recommended daily allowance is 300 mg.

If it's period pain that is cramping your style, the best painkillers are ibuprofen and naproxen sodium, both part of the non-steroidal anti-inflammatory drug family. And, hard as it may be to believe, researchers think that intense training eases period pain more effectively than more prolonged, gentler exercise. Try doing your hill training or speed work when you have period pain, to see whether this works for you. It may be that the endorphins released in response to exercise help mask the pain. Recent research from the University of Adelaide also found that women not only felt more sluggish early in their cycles, but they also burned less fat when they exercised earlier in the month.

why *we are here*

A recent British study (2002) found that vigorous exercise, such as running, two to three times a week resulted in a 25 per cent lower risk of all types of cancer – and a 62 per cent lower risk of cancers of the upper digestive tract.

making tracks 2

⠢ Absolute Beginners

GETTING UP AND RUNNING – A GUIDE FOR NEW RUNNERS

If this is your first foray into running, you are going to need at least six months to get yourself marathon-ready. Don't be tempted to pick a race sooner than that, even if you already participate in another sport, such as cycling or swimming, and have a good level of aerobic fitness – you will need to give your musculoskeletal system time to adapt to the specific demands of running. If you are a more experienced runner, you may want to skip this section.

The eight-week programme on page 16 aims to get you to a position where you can run continuously for 30 minutes. You don't have to follow the schedule to the letter, but it's a good template to ease you into regular running and offers a springboard to the 16-week marathon-specific programmes on pages 67–79.

You'll notice that there is a fair bit of walking involved in this programme. I am assuming that you can walk briskly for 30 minutes already, since you have set your sights, albeit distantly, on a marathon. If even walking for 30 minutes is a challenge, please put your marathon aspirations aside temporarily, and focus on improving your general fitness.

Having said that, far from being a cop-out, walking is an important component of a start-up running programme and, indeed, has a place in more experienced runners' schedules too. As you progress, it's simply a matter of gradually reducing the length of walking breaks, so that your running bouts get progressively longer. Stick with it and within eight weeks you should find yourself able to run continuously for 30 minutes. Only when you can run comfortably at a steady pace for 30 minutes or so should you begin to introduce other elements into your training, such as speed work or interval sessions. This is why it's crucial to follow this 'start-up' programme before you embark on marathon training and the different types of running it entails.

Getting off on the right foot

The number one beginner's mistake is to push too hard, too soon. This makes running a painful ordeal and a mission that is more likely to be abandoned. Although, not too long from now, there will be runs where I am actually encouraging you to run beyond your comfort zone, now is not that time. You should be running at a pace at which you can breathe without gasping and hold a conversation.

Each week there are three runs – but if you wish to repeat the first session to make four in total, then do so. (You will progress to the 30-minute goal faster.) Ensure you have a day's break between every run. The last run of the week is the 'challenge', which will eventually become your 'long run' when you are a fully-fledged marathon trainer.

Don't worry if you don't feel ready to cut down the walking intervals on the exact weeks stated or, indeed, if you feel more than ready to cut them down early – everyone progresses at different rates. Just don't try to run every day, or skip walking breaks by day three – make haste slowly.

Balancing act

Remember also to start every session with a warm-up (page 49), and finish with a cool down and stretch (pages 50–5). Start how you mean to go on! If you can find the time, follow the body maintenance workout on pages 59–62 to improve muscle strength and efficiency and reduce the risk of injury.

Week 1	Week 2	Week 3	Week 4
Walk for 3 minutes, run for 2 minutes and repeat 4 times (20 min)	Walk for 2 minutes, run for 2 minutes and repeat 6 times (24 min)	Walk for 1 minute, run for 3 minutes and repeat 6 times (24 min)	Walk for 1 minute, run for 4 minutes and repeat 5 times (25 min)
Walk for 3 minutes, run for 2 minutes and repeat 4 times (20 min)	Walk for 2 minutes, run for 2 minutes and repeat 6 times (24 min)	Walk for 1 minute, run for 3 minutes and repeat 6 times (24 min)	Walk for 1 minute, run for 4 minutes and repeat 5 times (25 min)
Challenge: Walk for 3 minutes, run for 2 minutes and repeat 5 times (25 min)	*Challenge:* Walk for 2 minutes, run for 3 minutes and repeat 5 times (25 min)	*Challenge:* Walk for 1 minute, run for 4 minutes and repeat 5 times (25 min)	*Challenge:* Jog for 10 minutes (walk as and when you need to), rest for 2 minutes and repeat (22 min)

Week 5	Week 6	Week 7	Week 8
Walk for 1 minute, run for 4 minutes and repeat 6 times (30 min)	Run for 8 minutes, walk for 1 minute and repeat 3 times (27 min)	Run for 10 minutes, walk for 30 seconds and repeat 3 times (31.5 min)	Run for 15 minutes, walk for 1 minute and repeat (32 min)
Walk for 1 minute, run for 4 minutes and repeat 6 times (30 min)	Run for 9 minutes, walk for 1 minute and repeat 3 times (30 min)	Run for 10 minutes, walk for 30 seconds and repeat 3 times (31.5 min)	Run for 15 minutes, walk for 30 seconds and repeat (31 min)
Challenge: Jog for 8 minutes, walk or rest for 1 minute and repeat two more times (27 min)	*Challenge:* Jog for 10 minutes, rest or walk for 30 seconds and repeat 3 times (31.5 min)	*Challenge:* Run for 15 minutes, walk or rest for 1 minute and repeat (32 min)	*Challenge:* Run for 30 minutes non-stop

∴ Perfect motion

THE IMPORTANCE OF GOOD TECHNIQUE – AND HOW TO ACHIEVE IT

Take a look at other runners when you're out pounding the pavements or jogging around the track at your local athletics club and you'll soon realise that, like dancing, everyone has their own individual style. Your running style is called your 'gait' and, although there are a number of things that may help you become a more relaxed and efficient runner, you shouldn't try to alter the way you run too much, or you may end up creating problems for yourself. Why? Because the body 'compensates' for its biomechanical imperfections and inadequacies, and your subsequent revised movement patterns may have been your natural way of moving for many years. Besides, many of the top runners in the world aren't textbook versions of perfection, but they still pull off amazing athletic achievements. This section takes a brief look at what constitutes good running technique and then goes on to suggest some ways of enhancing your own gait. First, though, a word about those oft-bandied-around words, pronation and supination. Many people say 'I pronate' to explain the fact that they wear orthotics, or have a specific pair of shoes on. But the truth is, we all pronate and supinate; it's all part of the gait cycle, and it's only when the pronation or supination phase is in some way dysfunctional that problems may arise.

Running gait – step by step

In spite of weird and wonderful individual variations, the general movement pattern that propels us forward is the same – you land on one foot (usually, though not always, on the outside edge of the mid-part of the heel), the muscles working eccentrically to decelerate the body and absorb shock. You then roll through the foot, the weight of the 'swing' leg providing the momentum for you to move forward, and the calves and hamstrings providing the muscle power to push off for the next stride. Each foot spends 40 per cent of its time in the air (swing phase) and 60 per cent on the ground (stance phase). When the foot lands, it rolls slightly in and forward, and the arch flattens to help dissipate the impact (this is the pronation bit). The knee then bends and the opposite leg pulls through, the body passing over the supporting foot to push off from the toes. By this time, the foot has moved into a 'supinated' position (the arch stiffens to give leverage) in which the pressure is predominantly on the outside edge of the foot, particularly on the big toe. A multitude of muscles are involved in this process with every step, both in stabilising the joints (for example, the deep stabilising muscles of the pelvis) and

facilitating forwards motion (the the larger calf muscle providing the power for toeing off).

Minor and major discrepancies in running gait can cause problems, although it's worth bearing in mind that they don't always. I know of runners who look as if they are an injury waiting to happen, yet who don't seem to incur any problems as a result of their running style. You can read more about avoiding injuries on pages 114–8 and about addressing them on pages 119–21. But first, let's look at the rules of 'good' running technique.

> *Many of the top runners in the world aren't textbook versions of perfection, but they still pull off amazing athletic achievements.*

Running techniques

Malcolm Balk, a Canadian running coach and Alexander Technique teacher, has developed a method of running which has helped many runners stay injury free, improve performance and get more enjoyment from their sport. Balk's 'Art of Running' uses Alexander Technique principles to help runners increase their kinaesthetic awareness and stop forcing and controlling their movement. Another technique that promises to reduce injuries and enhance performance by minimising wasting effort is the Pose Method, developed by Dr Nicholas Romanov, a Russian running coach now based in the United States. See 'Further Information' for more details.

Ten tips for better technique

 Relax – it's impossible to run well if you aren't relaxed. Pay attention to common tension sites, including the hands (unclench those fists), the jaw and forehead, and the shoulders. Research shows that when we clench the jaw, neural signals are sent along the spinal cord, causing us to 'brace' our posture and tense up.

 Let the knees, not the feet, lead the legs. Imagine your limbs moving in a circular motion, so that your foot lands under your knee rather than in front of it, where it will act as a 'brake'.

 Don't grip with the front of your ankles, particularly on hills. Many of us have a tendency to run with rigid ankles, which doesn't help with shock dissipation or a smooth stride. (Swimming can help loosen inflexible ankles.)

 Visualise growing taller with every step – this should help you avoid slumping on to the pelvis, a position in which your core stability is compromised. Running tall requires a certain amount of muscle strength and stability as well as know-how – see the 'Body Maintenance' workout on page 56 for more details.

 Don't try too hard. Running isn't a battle against the ground or the air. Imagine it as a controlled 'topple' forwards – all you need do is put your legs and arms out and you're on your way! Don't deliberately 'flick' off the toes as your foot leaves the ground or clench them inside your shoes. Land on the heel and roll smoothly through to the forefoot.

 You only need try running with your hands in your pockets to realise how much your arms count in running. Imagine they are pistons, propelling you forwards, with elbows bent to around 90 degrees. Don't allow the arms to swing across the body, and put most of the effort in on the forward swing, as the arm will spring back on its own.

 Your head weighs approximately 7–10 lb (depending on how clever you are!), so be smart and look ahead, not down, otherwise the weight of it will throw your upper spine forward and make your lower back to stick out/arch, putting a lot of stress on the skeleton. Focus on the ground 5–10 metres ahead. The other thing to avoid is allowing your head to jut out on your neck, a position many of us adopt sitting in front of a computer or TV, which worsens as we get tired.

 Run light – think of running over the ground rather than into it. Don't bounce from foot to foot.

 As mentioned above, clenched fists are not conducive to relaxed running, but that doesn't mean you should let your wrists and hands flop around randomly either. Runners are often advised to imagine they are holding a crisp between each thumb and forefinger, tight enough to hold it without crushing it. I prefer to let my thumbs curl in to my palms, but in a 'relaxed clench' position.

 Monitor yourself as you run. Practise running through a 'body scan' from top to toe. Are you gritting your teeth, or are your arms coming across your body? Take a quick scan, take note of any tension, tightness or pain, then regroup and carry on.

Stride and tested

How fast you run is a product of how big your stride is and how many steps you take. The more steps you take and the bigger your strides, the faster you will be. Makes sense, huh? But which is most important? This is one of those areas in which the experts simply can't agree. You'll often hear that, since your stride length is largely determined by leg length and flexibility, increasing the number of steps – your turnover – is the best way to speed up. However, research suggests that getting someone to run at a particular pace and then asking them to speed up results in a far bigger stride and only a very small increase in stride frequency. For example, in one study, doubling speed from 10 to 20 kph increased stride length by 85 per cent and stride frequency by only 9 per cent.

Then again, in experiments in which runners instinctively pick their most economical stride length, and are then asked to increase or decrease it, they have to work harder and use more oxygen. So it may be counterproductive to consciously aim to extend your stride. Perhaps the best way ahead is to ensure that your stride is optimal by practising good technique and flexibility, keeping feet 'fast and light,' and trying some of the drills overleaf.

Uphill technique

The most common mistake runners make when taking to the hills is to look down, taking the hefty weight of the head forward and throwing the spine out of alignment. Leaning forward also reduces the involvement of the hamstrings, giving you less propulsion. Instead, look ahead, shorten your stride a little and use your arms to help propel you upwards. Don't try to maintain the same pace you had on flat ground. The golden rule is 'even effort, not even pace'.

Downhill technique

Running downhill might sound a lot easier than running uphill, but the knees and quads can take a real pounding, not just because of the increased impact but because the thigh muscles are contracting eccentrically (to decelerate you), which causes more microtrauma (microscopic damage) in the muscle. To descend less painfully, relax, particularly in the thighs and at the front of the ankles, and don't 'brake' or lean backwards. Take your arms wider for balance, but ensure you don't inadvertently take legs wider, too. Don't look down – it's tempting to do so if you are running on rough trail, but try to pick your route a few metres ahead and then keep your eyes focused on the next bit of trail instead of on your feet.

Breathe easy

There are lots of 'theories' on the best way to breathe during running. I believe the best way is the way that comes most naturally. I am not a proponent of all these 'breathe in for two strides, out for two strides'-patterns, or of advising runners to breathe in through the nose and out through the mouth. A study from Liverpool John Moores University showed that once exercise is just moderately hard, the most efficient way of breathing in and out is through the mouth, not the nose – and besides, for much of the summer, my nose is way too blocked up to breathe through any way, and the only true advantage I can see is that I don't swallow quite so many flies....

why we are here

Danish researchers looked at 4,600 men aged 20–79, over a 5-year period, and found that regular joggers were 63 per cent less likely to die early than inactive guys. Running 20 miles a week is thought to increase life expectancy by at least two years.

Technique drills – as easy as 1,2,3

1 Bounding

Bounding improves explosive power, increases stride length and boosts bone density in the hips. In an exaggerated running stride, leap from foot to foot, swinging your arms and raising your knees high with each step. Aim for 4–5 x 10 bounds.

2 Heel flicks

Heel Flicks increase range of motion at the hip and knee, strengthen hamstrings and challenge core stability. It's important that the knees and thighs are raised in front of the torso, rather than staying underneath it. Start on the spot, flicking your heels up towards your bottom while simultaneously bringing your knees up slightly in front. Do not lean back. Once you've got the action going, move forward.
Go for 2–3 x 20 metres.

3 Strides/pick-ups

Strides are a slightly slower version of a sprint, and will help improve your running form and extend your range of motion. The greater 'drive' required by the supporting leg as it pushes off also puts more emphasis on the hamstrings, while the forefoot landing strengthens the calves. From a standing start, begin to run and gradually speed up to a pace just below your sprint speed. Go for 5 x 20 metres.

⁂ The truth about training

WHY RUNNING THE SAME PACE, SAME DISTANCE, SAME ROUTE DAY AFTER DAY WON'T GET YOU ROUND THE MARATHON

Ask anyone who's run a marathon, and they'll probably tell you that the hardest part isn't the 26.2-mile run itself – it's the training. There's no denying that there's some hard graft to be done between now and marathon day, but knowing what to do, how and when to do it, and why you're doing it goes some way towards making the task easier. It gives every training session a point, rather than simply being more miles to note in your training log.

Just running for the sake of it – mile after mile at the same speed, covering the same distance around the same route is pretty boring for even the most committed runner – and it certainly won't help you reach your marathon potential. To understand why, let's have a look at the principles of training, and how they relate to going the distance.

Progressive overload

When you take your first faltering steps on the road to marathon fitness, you will find that you progress in leaps and bounds. The run that felt like a near-death experience in week one will barely have you breaking a sweat in a couple of months' time. Sadly, though, this doesn't mean that training gets easier and easier as you go along. What it means is that as you reach each new level of fitness you need to increase the challenge to your body – effectively moving the goalposts further away. Why? Because your body will continue to adapt and get fitter only when the challenge placed upon it is greater than that which it can already handle. This is a principle known as 'progressive overload'. 'Overload', because it relates to the amount of work or 'stress' you place on your body, and 'progressive' because piling on the workload all at once simply won't work. You must make haste slowly to ensure success without injury, illness or burnout.

Reversibility

In the same way that the body adapts to the stimulus of training, if you stop training, all your hard-earned gains are soon lost! If you reach a 'comfort zone', and fail to increase the speed, distance or frequency of your runs, further adaptation will cease and you could end up falling short of the physiological changes your body needs to complete the marathon. A study by scientists in Sweden found that after only six days of rest, up to 10 per cent of aerobic capacity had been lost. That doesn't mean to say that you should never take a day's rest – recovery is a crucial ingredient of a training programme (see below) – but the sad fact is, you can't store fitness.

Recovery

If you think marathon training has to mean seven days a week, maximum effort every time, you are

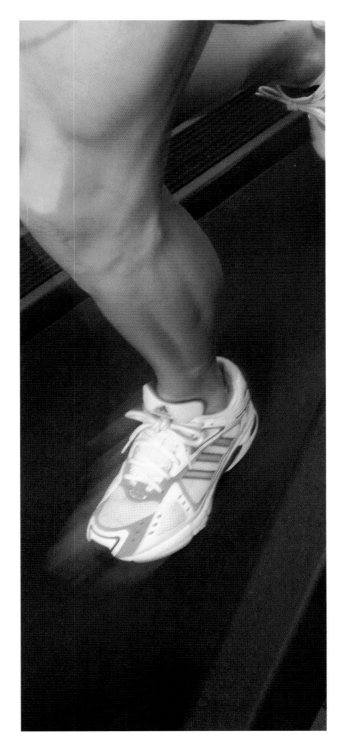

mistaken. Such a regime will leave you stale, fatigued, ill or injured, and you'll never achieve the performance you are capable of. Why? Because your training regime is missing one essential, but often overlooked, element – rest! Recovery time is when the body undergoes the physiological adaptations that the training has stimulated. Take it away, and you would never be giving your body chance to develop, and never giving any minor injuries or ailments chance to heal. When it comes to marathon training, 'no pain – no gain' and 'if some is good, more must be better' are definitely not appropriate mantras to be chanting.

Specificity

The adaptations your body makes as a result of progressive overload are based on the type of training you do. What does that mean? That to get better at a particular type of activity, you need to do that activity. That's why swimmers swim, climbers climb, dancers dance and runners run. While your heart neither knows nor cares whether you're dancing the tango or out for a steady jog (it's all cardiovascular exercise, after all), being specific about the type of exercise you do is the best way of developing the muscles, tendons and ligaments – as well as the neuromuscular patterns – that are going to be needed for your event. However, that doesn't mean there isn't scope for runners to include some different types of training into their programme, just that the core part of the training programme for a marathon has to be running.

The F.I.T. principle

OK, so you know you need to run, that you need to progressively increase the challenge of your runs, and that you need to schedule in some rest days, but not too many. So far, so good. This final principle – represented by the acronym F.I.T – is about getting down to the nitty-gritty. In real terms, F.I.T. relates to how often, how hard and how long should you run?

'F' stands for frequency. How often are you going to run?

'I' stands for intensity. How much effort are you going to put in to your run?

'T' stands for time. How long are you going to run for? Or how far are you going to go?

It is important to vary both the intensity and distance of your runs, in order to work on different elements of fitness. While on the big day itself you'll be running at a fairly constant, less-than-maximal pace for a prolonged period, that doesn't mean it should be the only way you train. In order to prime the muscular and cardiovascular systems optimally, you need to work at a variety of effort levels.

However, when it comes to the F.I.T. trio, there is a vital rule: when you increase one variable, the others should stay constant. For example, if you work harder, don't try to work longer too. If you add in another weekly run, don't try to increase the length of your existing runs. Why? Because that doesn't represent 'progressive overload' – it's simply 'overload'. Research from Ball State University found that most runners need 48–72 hours to recover fully from even a moderately hard session, which is why it's vital to follow tough training days with easy ones.

Getting to grips with pace

There are a couple of ways of determining the intensity you are working at. One is to use a heart rate monitor, which you can read about on page 43. Alternatively, you can use your 'rate of perceived exertion' (RPE) to gauge your effort. The benefit of RPE is that it is truly individual. One person's conversation pace may be another's near-maximal speed. Also, as you get fitter, your pace will quicken, so you'll be able to run at, say, your level 2, a little bit faster.

The RPE scale in this book ranges from 1–5. The marathon training programmes on pages 67–79 relate to these effort levels, and a heart rate range is indicated for each one. Find out how to determine your heart rate ranges on page 26.

Rate your running here!

Effort level 1

Easy pace. Use this pace during the 'recovery' sections of your interval training and fartlek, or for a very easy run. Equates to 60–65 per cent max heart rate.

Effort level 2

Conversation pace. Use this pace on your steady runs. Equates to 65–75 per cent of max heart rate.

Effort level 3

Challenging pace. Use this pace on your threshold runs. Equates to 75–85 per cent max heart rate.

Effort level 4

Tough pace. Use this pace on hill work and longer speed repetitions or interval training. Equates to 85–90 per cent max heart rate.

Effort level 5

Maximal pace. Use this pace on shorter speed reps (for example, 200 m) and intervals only – with rests at least twice as long as the length of the effort. Equates to 90 per cent plus of your max heart rate.

Now you know about the principles of training and the demands of the marathon, we can take a look at the different types of run involved in working at these different paces or intensities, and what place they might hold in your marathon training programme.

Heart rate basics

If you need to be working at, say, 75 per cent of your maximum heart rate, you first need to know what that maximum heart rate is. You can have this measured in a laboratory (see 'Further Information' on page 173), but a simpler option is to use one of the two following formulas.

The 220 – age formula
Subtract your age from 220 to get an estimated maximum heart rate value. (Research has shown that true values can be as much as 20 beats out, however.) Example: you are 35 years old; so 220 – 35 = 185. Now simply work out the heart rate corresponding to 65 per cent, 70 per cent or 75 per cent of it. Example: 75 per cent of 185 = 139 bpm

The Karvonen formula
For this, you need to know your resting heart rate (see page 5) and your age-determined or actual maximum heart rate. Results are more accurate. Example: you are 40 years old. Your resting heart rate is 70 bpm, your age-related maximum heart rate is 180 and you want to know what your heart rate would be working at 70 per cent of your maximum.
70% = (MHR – RHR) x 70% + RHR
70% = (180 – 70) x 70% + RHR
70% = 110 x 70% = 77 + 70
70% = 147bpm

Don't give up

Becoming a runner isn't easy – there will be times when your old, sedentary lifestyle beckons, when the weather is foul and you can't bear to drag yourself out the door, and when the aches and pains hardly seem worth it. But keep going! You'll find tips on staying motivated on page 89–91. Rest assured, a few weeks from now you will begin to reap the benefits of a healthier lifestyle, a fitter body and a more focused mind. And then you'll be ready for your marathon journey.

❖ Way to go

THE LOWDOWN ON DIFFERENT TYPES OF RUN AND THEIR BENEFITS FOR MARATHON TRAINING

There are many ways to run – long and slow, short and fast, repetitive bursts of hard efforts, up hills, down hills and on all manner of different surfaces. None is bad, all of them work (in terms of improving fitness), but some are more effective for marathon training than others. Which ones?

Before trying to answer that question, it is important to realise that running is not an 'exact' science, unlike engineering or nuclear physics. There is no completely right or totally wrong way of training – but certain ways of training will optimise the time that you have available, and lead to the best returns from your training miles. For example, you'll need to include plenty of long runs in your training programme. A study by scientists from Hong Kong looked at factors predicting the successful completion of a marathon and found that the single most important indicator was the length of the competitor's longest training run. This was even more important than total weekly mileage and the number of marathons already run. The long run develops endurance, but you also need strength and – believe it or not – speed. It's all too easy for marathon runners to focus only on long, steady running, without reaping the benefits that can be gained from honing strength and speed. Researchers from Sweden have found that the best way to increase the volume of the heart is through steady, long distance runs, whereas the best way to increase the strength and thickness of the heart walls is by more intensive runs. This represents the perfect example of why you need to vary your training to get the results you want.

The long run

What is it? A prolonged, steady-paced session.

Why do it? The long run is, without doubt, the most important training session for budding marathoners. As well as proffering great physiological benefits, such as increased blood volume, improved oxygen extraction from the blood (due to more capillaries), enhanced fat utilisation, calorie expenditure, stronger connective tissue and greater muscular endurance, the long run will develop the mind-set and willpower that you'll need to keep going, and give you confidence that you can beat the marathon distance.

How do I do it? Set aside one weekly session to include to a long run. 'Long' is a relative term. If you are a beginner, then long may mean only 30 minutes, but the crucial thing is to extend it each time, to your chosen peak distance. Run at Effort Level 2 – at first you will probably be at the lower end of this effort level, but as the training weeks pass try to work a little harder, to mimic the pace you hope to run at in the race itself. This normally equates to 70–75 per cent of your maximum heart rate. The distance or 'time on your feet' increases by 1–2 miles per week in the marathon training programmes on pages 67–79, with the odd week off to consolidate, or to try a race.

Try this: If you are daunted by the long run, adopt a walk-run strategy to help give you the confidence you need to be on your feet for prolonged periods. An ideal walk-run ratio for marathon training is 8 minutes running (at Effort Level 2 or 65–75 per cent maximum heart rate), 2 minutes walking (it's also easy to keep track of on your sports watch). Gradually reduce the walking breaks until they disappear altogether.

Steady runs/easy runs

What is it? Exactly what it says on the tin. A steady-paced run that isn't as long as your long run. In an 'easy run' or 'recovery run', the pace and distance are even lower.

Why do it? Steady runs are what I think of as my 'sanity runs'. They aren't long or fast enough to be daunting; they are simply enjoyable training miles, run at a pace that will improve heart health, oxygen delivery to the muscles, fat utilisation and muscular endurance. At the lower end of the scale, 'easy' or 'recovery' runs are a way of encouraging adaptation from tougher sessions by speeding up the recovery process, clearing waste products from the muscles and getting time on your feet without putting in too much effort.

How do I do it? Steady runs should be run at Effort Level 2 – conversation pace, but at the upper edge of your comfort zone, rather than slap bang in the middle of it. This is the pace you are building up to in your long run (see above) and is achievable now because the distance isn't so great. For easy/recovery runs, the crucial thing is to ensure that the pace really is easy. Run at Effort Level 1, (around 60–65 per cent MHR) at a relatively constant pace, allowing for slight variations in work rate for hills and changes in terrain.

Try this: 30–50 minute steady-paced run at 70–75 per cent MHR or at what you would consider to be Effort Level 2.5.

Threshold training

What is it? A swift run at a pace that has you teetering on the brink of your lactate or anaerobic threshold (see box on page 30). This isn't a pace at which you'll feel comfortable chatting, but thankfully it won't last too long – usually between 20 and 30 minutes. Sometimes threshold training is known as 'tempo running'.

Why do it? Working at an intensity that equates to the lactate threshold will gradually push it upwards, so that you can produce energy aerobically at a higher intensity. It also gets your body accustomed to exercising with lactic acid in the muscles (improving lactate tolerance) and to clearing lactate acid from the muscles more efficiently. A group of French scientists who monitored high-standard runners during a six-week training programme that included threshold runs found that the runners experienced significant physiological improvements in aerobic capacity, resulting in up to two minutes off 10km time. The other essential pay-off from threshold running is an improvement in leg turnover speed and running economy.

How do I do it? Threshold runs should be run at Effort Level 3, or 75–85 per cent of your maximum heart rate. Determining your threshold pace isn't easy unless you have access to a high-tech physiology laboratory (see 'Further Information') – you should just about be able to hold a very abbreviated conversation, and be running at the sort of speed you can sustain for a 20–30 minute run.

Try this: To get yourself into the swing of threshold running, split your session into two: run at threshold pace for 15 minutes, rest for 2 minutes, and then repeat.

Tip: As a break from a standard threshold run, try breaking it down into 1 km efforts at threshold pace, with a 60-second recovery between each one. Try for 3–5 km.

Interval training

What is it? A run in which you intersperse fast efforts of running with periods of recovery. The intensity (speed at which the effort is run), length of the effort (either distance or time), length of the recovery interval and volume (number of efforts) can all be changed to suit the needs of the runner and ensure progression in the programme.

Why do it? A study published in the *Journal of Sports Medicine and Physical Fitness* found 6 per cent improvements in VO$_2$ max (see box on page 31) among recreational runners after just six weeks of interval training. As well as boosting endurance, faster running will improve leg turnover and strength and get you accustomed to working at a higher heart rate and effort level. Interval running will enable you to put in a good deal of quality work without completely exhausting you or being psychologically daunting, thanks to those recovery periods.

How do I do it? The number of intervals that can be completed will depend on your level of fitness, and the intensity and length of the effort. A session focusing on building speed endurance should allow less time to recover than a session focusing on pure speed, relatively speaking. For example, if you ran a 1 km interval, you might take 1.5 to 2 minutes to recover before setting off again. If, however, you ran 400 m, you might take 2 to 3 minutes to recover. This is for two reasons: first, you'll be completing the 400 m reps a lot faster than you will the 1 km reps; second, if you are looking to boost speed, as with the shorter session, you need to allow the body to recover completely each time, while in the former session the onus is on improving endurance, so a full recovery isn't necessary. If you feel tired halfway through an interval session, slow down the pace of the run rather than increasing the length of the recovery period.

Try this: 4 to 5 3-minute efforts with a 2-minute recovery jog or walk between each one. The 3-minute bouts should be run at Effort Level 4, and the recovery at Effort Level 1. French research suggests that this is the optimal way to develop aerobic capacity.

Fartlek

What is it? 'Fartlek' running has its origins in

What's all this about lactate threshold?

When sufficient oxygen is flowing through the bloodstream to meet energy needs, such as at an easy running pace, the mitochondria or 'engine rooms' in the muscle cells can use it to produce energy with minimal fuss and effort. But when there isn't enough oxygen coming through to meet demand – such as when you are exercising heavily, the muscle cells have to produce energy without oxygen, or anaerobically. This is far less efficient, since it results in the accumulation of heat and a substance called lactic acid, which makes the muscle very acidic and hampers muscular contraction. The lactic acid is continually being removed, but if it is produced at a faster rate than it can be taken away, then it builds up in the muscle and, before you know it, you've crossed the 'lactate threshold', (also sometimes called the anaerobic threshold). Physiologically, the lactate threshold is the last point at which lactate is being removed as fast as it is being produced. Running at a pace which is equal to this point effectively pushes the threshold upwards, so you can run faster without crossing it.

Scandinavia, and is eally just a less structured version of interval running. Translated, the term means 'speed play', and it simply involves runners putting in faster or harder bursts when they feel ready, during a steady run (often on mixed terrain and inclines).

Why do it? Fartlek training is a great way of easing yourself into faster running without it seeming too intimidating. It's basically a way of increasing the intensity of a steady run, without increasing the distance, (we're back to overload again), and can also add a bit of variety to what might be an all too familiar run around a well-troddencourse. Fartlek training will soon start to trigger the physiological adaptations needed to complete 26.2 miles – and will make running at a constant pace seem much easier.

How do I do it? Set off at a steady pace and then use landmarks, such as lamp posts, trees, or the coun down function on your stopwatch, to put in a faster effort. You can also use the terrain to dictate the intensity of the run – by running fast up a hill, and jogging until you have recovered. You don't have to make it too formal, but have a general idea of how many efforts you are going to put in from the start.

Try this: A 45-minute run at Effort Level 2 that includes 12 periods of faster running at Effort Levels 3–5 (depending on the length of the effort, of course!), between 30 seconds and 2 minutes long. Try to alternate between longer and shorter bursts.

Speed work

What is it? Speed training is about running fast – way faster than you intend to run that marathon. It is traditionally done on an athletics track, but doesn't have to be – although it's best to find somewhere flat and even for your speed work.

Why do it? Even as an endurance runner, speed is an essential piece of the training jigsaw, and will elevate your fitness more than you'd believe. It will also improve your running technique, your leg strength and power, and your 'economy' (your ability to run faster at any given heart rate), one of the key factors in successful marathon running according to a report in *Sports Medicine* in 2001. Speed training makes slower-paced running seem much easier, and helps you develop a 'sprint finish' for race day. It certainly won't be the main part of your training – it puts a lot of stress on the body and is the kind of session in which you are more vulnerable to injury, but an occasional speed fest is well worthwhile.

How do I do it? Little and often. Speed work shouldn't be tackled until you have a good level of leg strength,

built up through steady running, hill training and Fartlek. The efforts should be at Level 4–5, depending on the distance being covered and the recovery periods.

Try this: Four x 400 m efforts, separated by 120 seconds rest. Jog for five minutes, then repeat.

Tip: Remember to pace yourself when you are doing speed 'reps'. It's a mistake to think that speed work means sprinting. It doesn't. The mark of a successful speed session is when all your reps are roughly the same length of time, or slightly faster. If you do your first 800 m in 2.55 and the rest at just under 4 minutes, then you started out too fast.

VO$_2$ max for beginners

The maximum rate at which oxygen can be extracted from the air and used by the muscle is called your maximal oxygen uptake, or VO$_2$ max. It is largely determined by your genetics (as well as sex, age and body size) but that doesn't mean you can't improve it through regular training (most of us are far from our genetic potential). Studies suggest we can increase VO$_2$ max by 5–25 per cent through exercise. As a general example, a sedentary man may have a VO$_2$ max of 30 ml/kg/min while a highly trained man may be closer to 70 ml/kg/min.

why we are here

Being a runner makes you sexier! Not just because you've got a lithe, toned body, but because you're more sexually responsive. An American study of 8,000 women aged 18–49 found that of those who exercised three times a week, 40 per cent reported greater arousal, 31 per cent had sex more often and 25 per cent found orgasm easier to achieve.

Hill training

What is it? A hill session is one that uses gravity to add to the overload on your body. While any run that takes in undulating territory could be considered 'hill training', a hill session is usually more structured, doing 'repeats' on one particular hill.

Why do it? Even if your marathon is flat, it is worth including some hill work because you'll have to work harder to overcome the extra resistance that gravity causes, developing the muscles, ligaments and tendons and enhancing cardiovascular fitness. In a study from the University of Georgia in Greece, scientists monitored a group of athletes during both level and uphill running, and found that there was over 20 per cent more activation of the muscle fibres on hills.

How do I do it? Choose a hill that has a gentle gradient if you are new to this kind of training, a moderate gradient if you're a more experienced runner but not more than 10 per cent. Forget about Everest-style inclines, your technique will suffer too much for it to be beneficial. Run up the hill at a swift pace (Effort Level 3–4), jogging back down to recover, and running straight back up. It's important to run off the top of the hill rather than allow yourself to slow down when the peak is in sight.

Try this: Find a road with a longish gradual hill (say, up to a 2-minute climb) and lamp posts or rubbish bins for markers. Start at the bottom and run at a swift pace to the first marker, then recover by jogging back to the bottom. Next run to the second lamp post, and so on, until you reach the top, then work your way back down again in the same manner. You can also use the incline on a treadmill for your hill sessions.

Downhill running

While not a bona fide running session in its own right, there is a place for downhill running in your training, even if you are not going to be making descents on race day. A slight decline enables you to work on your leg turnover with less resistance, and is a good training aid that strengthens the legs and improves speed. If you *are* going to be running lots of descents on race day you must practise in training, since downhill running puts a lot of stress on the muscle fibres, due to the high proportion of eccentric muscle contraction involved. This type of muscle contraction is known to lead to a greater strengthening of the muscles, but at the same time can cause significant muscle soreness up to 48 hours later, so make sure you avoid doing too much too close to an important training session or race.

Try this: Within a steady run or fartlek session, try 6 to 8 200 m runs down a gentle slope, jogging back up to the top to recover. Aim for a brisk pace, concentrating on good form, but don't sprint.

Hills, reps, fartlek, steady runs...how does it all fit into a budding marathoner's training week? Find out by checking out the programmes on pages 67–79. But first, we're going shopping....

∵ Going shopping

THE SHOES, KIT AND GADGETS YOU NEED TO GET STARTED

This section is devoted to my favourite activity (other than running, of course), shopping. First we'll look at the basics – running shoes and kit and then check out some useful extras...

They are likely to ask you...

❧ Can I take a look at/measure your feet?

❧ How many miles/hours a week do you/will you train?

❧ How heavy are you?

❧ Do you/have you had any injury problems?

❧ What is your budget?

❧ Where do you train (terrain)?

If they don't ask you any of these questions, and simply try to sell you the most expensive pair of running shoes they stock, take your custom elsewhere....

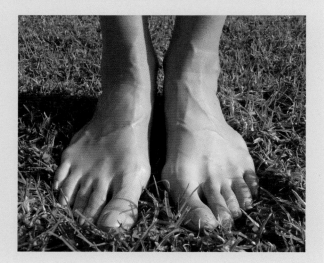

Running shoes

First things first – running shoes. Since a force equal to at least two to three times your body weight is produced every time your foot hits the ground (and that's at a steady running speed on the flat), shoes that absorb impact and offer protection are vital. According to US health and fitness organisation, IDEA, poor arch support can lead to plantar fascitis, inadequate heel cushioning can lead to heel spurs, and insufficient shock absorption can increase the risk of lower leg stress fractures and lower back pain. To maximise comfort and performance and minimise the risk of injury, then, you need the right shoe.

Nowadays, there are shoes to suit all shapes, sizes, biomechanical differences and budgets. Even for the most experienced of runners, the choice can be mind-boggling. The best solution is to visit a specialist sports or running shop that stocks a wide range of brands and has knowledgeable staff.

why *we are here*

Research published in the journal *Arthritis and Rheumatism* shows that running can protect against osteoarthritis by keeping joints and connective tissue strong, mobile and topped up with nutrients. A recent study from Stanford University found that regular long-term runners are 25 per cent less likely to suffer from osteoarthritis than sedentary people.

What to look for in a running shoe

You need to be prepared to spend at least £50 for a reputable brand and model. Think of it like this: good shoes might not last longer than cheaper shoes but, like investing in a good quality paint, you'll get a better finish. First and foremost consideration, when buying your first pair of running shoes, is comfort. It doesn't matter if it's the latest, greatest most expensive model in the shop, if it doesn't feel comfy, don't buy it. And certainly don't expect to 'wear it in'. Trainers should feel good straight away – the acid test is if you can wear them for the first time and forget that they are new.

Comfort also means fit. There should be the width of your index finger between your longest toe and the end of the shoe. Don't buy a size 8 just because all your shoes are a size 8. If size 8 or even size 9 feels better, opt for that. Different brands come up very differently in size, both in length and width.

The second most important consideration is stability. Stability, or 'motion control', is determined by the structure of the shoe, particularly the mid-sole, (the heart of the shoe) where all the technical features are housed. Stability features, such as a medial post (an insert of high-density foam or plastic), will 'steady' your foot as it lands, to prevent excessive pronation.

Finally, shock absorption, or cushioning, is also important. A study published in the *International Journal of Sports Medicine* concluded that shoe cushioning could reduce the effect of impact forces on spinal structures – so it's not just your feet you are protecting. Shock absorbing material may come in the form of an air capsule, foam or gel, and what you are looking at is what type of absorption is on offer, and where in the shoe it is placed.

The Ten Commandments of shoe shopping

1 Thou shalt never EVER buy cross-trainers or shoes designed for anything other than running in place of designated running shoes.

2 Thou shalt shop for trainers in the afternoon or, even better, after a run, when your feet are slightly bigger.

3 Thou shalt stand, not sit, when assessing the amount of space in the front of the shoe. You need approximately 1/4 inch beyond your longest toe (which is not always the big toe).

4 Thou shalt try on both shoes together. Everyone has one foot slightly larger than the other.

5 Thou shalt be particularly picky about the fit around the heel. A study from the University of Illinois showed that a poor-fitting heel cup (too loose) could cause ankle and knee problems.

6 Thou shalt expect instant comfort. If the shoe doesn't feel great as soon as you put it on, don't buy it.

7 Thou shalt run at least a few steps in the shoes, either around or outside the shop or on a treadmill (provided for this purpose).

8 Thou shalt not be seduced by gimmicks. Even the biggest, most famous shoe companies have introduced 'revolutionary' technology to their brands that have fallen flat.

9 Thou shalt wear sports socks and, if you have them, orthotics, when you are trying on shoes.

10 When thou hast found the perfect running shoe, thou shalt go back and buy another pair. At least one. Shoe manufacturers have an annoying habit of changing models year in, year out.

Determining your foot type and shoe needs

Trace and match

Shoes are built on something called a 'last', which is basically a foot-shaped mould. Different shoe brands use different shaped lasts – some have a squarer toe box, while others are more rounded; some allow for a wider forefoot than others. Since your foot is going to go inside the shoe, it is reasonable to assume that the two should be roughly the same shape, so trace your bare foot, cut it out and take the tracing with you when you go shoe shopping, to match to the shape of the insole or outsole.

Make a wet footprint

The imprint your foot leaves gives an idea of whether you have particularly high- or low-arched feet, which may affect your gait. Dip your feet in water and then walk across a flat, even surface, such as concrete, hard sand or even a sheet of cardboard. Can you see the entire silhouette of your foot or is it more of an outline, with just heels and toes showing?

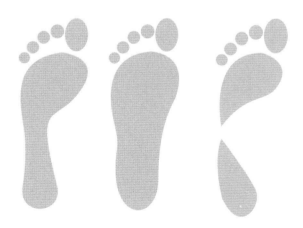

- Toes and forefoot plus heel show, joined by a broad band: indicates normal or 'neutral' footstrike.

- Entire foot shows: indicates low or flat arches, associated with overpronation.

- Toe prints plus heel but little in between: indicates high arches, which are associated with excessive supination, or underpronation.

Get adidas FootScanned

The adidas *FootScan* machine is installed in a number of specialist running shops across the UK. It uses digital imaging to create a 'picture' of your foot, showing where most of the pressure goes when your foot lands (telling you, for example, if you are a forefoot striker, or whether you have more pressure on your right foot than your left). You stand, and then run, on a pressure-sensitive mat while the *FootScan* records your foot's movements at a rate of 500 frames per second and then constructs a digital image, which can be used to determine the best type of shoe for your needs. The service is provided free of charge.

Go for analysis

Gait analysis is quite the thing is running circles nowadays, but is it really necessary? The answer is yes, if you have had any previous knee, back or hip injuries or problems; yes, if you already know you have an abnormal gait or foot mechanics; and possibly yes, if you have recently had a baby and are returning to running. As far as the rest of us are concerned, the usefulness of gait analysis is debatable. While some sports medicine experts believe that it is an essential preventative measure to detect faults before they become problematic, others believe the old adage 'if it ain't broke, don't fix it'.

What happens in gait analysis?

Gait analysis should be conducted by a podiatrist, biomechanist or physiotherapist. The consultation will start with some questions about your general health, any joint or muscular problems, past injuries and your current running regime. The consultant will then take a look at your posture in standing and assess the function of some important 'stabilising' muscles. Then you'll hop on to the treadmill (usually barefoot at first) and you'll be videoed walking and running. Ideally, you'll also be analysed in your running footwear, too. Afterwards, the practitioner will take you through the video, showing you frame by frame where any problems lie. You may be given exercises to do to improve the strength and function of particular muscles, and you may be prescribed orthotics. These are special insoles that go inside the shoe to enable the body to correct faulty movement patterns. Off-the-peg orthoses, which cost under £100, may help if you have a very minor biomechanical problem, but custom-made ones, designed to cope with more serious problems, can cost £300 or more, although they do last a lifetime. See 'Further Information' for details on gait analysis and podiatry.

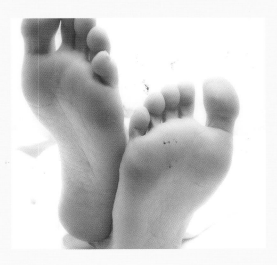

Maintenance and replacement

Running shoes don't last forever. In fact, if you count miles, 300 to 500 miles (depending on how heavy you are and the type of surface you run on) is considered the average life span. Even if there are no signs of wear, you should replace running shoes after 500 miles of use (depending on your speed – that's between 50 and 70 hours' running). To maximise their life, keep your running shoes for running, rather than wearing them for the gym and other activities, never wear them without socks (especially if you want to keep some friends), and don't put them in the washing machine. It's also a good idea to rotate two different pairs of running shoes. The mid-sole is compressed during running and takes up to 24 hours to return to normal. If your trainers are muddy, wet or smelly, remove the insoles and use a brush and water to clean the insoles and uppers – leave them to dry naturally in a warm but not hot place (too much heat will melt the glue that holds them together).

Trail shoes

If a significant amount of your training is likely to take place off-road, it's worth considering investing in a pair of trail shoes. Since you'll be running on softer, more slippery and less stable surfaces, trail shoes will give you more grip (traction), thanks to lots of knobbly bits (lugs) on the out-sole of the shoe that grip without slipping. The upper part of the shoe will usually be reinforced, too, to protect your toes from rocks and tree roots – many are now water-resistant, too.

RUNNING SHOE ANATOMY

Heel tab

Insole

Upper

Laces

Toe box

Heel counter or cup

Midsole

Outsole

Lug

Socks

Simple? Yes. Inexpensive? Yes. Potential for disaster, if wrong? Huge! If you're regularly active and still buy three pairs of cotton sports socks for a tenner, you're missing out on the technical fabrics and features of the true performers, such as an absence of seams, or flat-stitched seams that don't chafe and cause blisters, sweat-wicking fabrics with anti-fungal properties, two-layer construction, better shaping (socks marked 'left' and 'right', no less) and even extra cushioning at the points of impact.

A good pair of socks needs to be absorbent, since your feet will produce large quantities of sweat when running, but the sweat then needs to be wicked away from the feet in order to prevent blisters and chafing. Cotton socks, while absorbing moisture efficiently, aren't able to do anything with it, so they cause the fabric to swell and create friction. Manmade fibres are a much better bet, maintaining their shape and fit, and keeping runners' feet drier.

Running kit

Not so long ago, you had to choose between fashion and function when buying running kit but, happily, that's no longer the case and there are some great ranges out there that have all the sweat-wicking, non-chafing, wind- and waterproofing properties, as well as the good looks. But what are the essentials? That depends on the time of year and climate in which you are going to be doing most of your training, so I have divided kit into winter and summer options. In general, as with socks, you should opt for manmade fabrics rather than cotton. Technical fabrics are able to wick moisture away from the skin over 50 per cent faster than cotton. Layering thin garments is better than opting for one big thick layer, since sweat can move more easily between two thin layers than it can through one thick one.

Kitting yourself out in the right gear will certainly make you feel the part, but there is also a comfort and convenience factor not to be sniffed at: ease of movement, better ventilation, reflective strips for safety and pockets for on-the-run items such as keys and coins.

Knot a problem

You've got perfect fit in the forefoot but your heel is slipping around. What to do? Adjust the laces. Do a 'normal' criss-cross lacing pattern up to the last-but-one hole. Then thread each end of the lace through the last hole on its own side, pulling a little bit of lace up to create a loop. Now take the end of each lace to the loop on the opposite side and pull tight. Problem solved!

Spring and summer running kit essentials

Bottom half

Running shorts: these are the lightest and coolest thing to run in, and since they aren't baggy, like football or basketball shorts, they won't flap around and chafe the inner thighs.

OR

Cycling shorts: good if you feel self conscious about skimpy running shorts, and providing extra insulation on cooler days.

OR

Lightweight, breathable long pants: particularly good if you frequently include trail runs in your weekly regime and need protection from nettles, brambles and ticks. Look for shorts with an inner support lining, internal key pockets, anti-microbial gussets (a godsend if you are prone to yeast infections), reflective strips and protected seams or external drawstrings around the waist to prevent chafing around the navel.

Top half

Sports bra: no woman should set foot out the door without a proper sports bra. Read all about why, and how to find the right one, in the box.

Vest: a running vest must fit perfectly – too loose and you will be continually hoisting the shoulder straps back on, too tight, and you will not get a cool flow of air around the chest and may end up suffering from soreness under the armpits.

OR

T-shirt: look for fabrics such as Coolmax and DriFIT (both trade names for polyester fabrics). Lycra adds better shape and fit. Don't go for one that's too baggy, or it will simply get in the way and increase air resistance.

Hat/visor: running in a hat in hot weather isn't advisable, since it prevents heat escaping through your head, but to protect your face, a visor, or a very lightweight, breathable baseball cap is a good option

Essential chick kit

Even an A-sized breast moves nearly half a centimetre away from the body during impact exercise (just think how much a D-cup moves). This movement, in a figure-of-eight type pattern, causes the supportive Cooper's ligaments to stretch, and can cause discomfort. A sports bra will minimise movement and make exercise more comfortable. There are two main styles. 'Encapsulated' bras separate and support each breast in its own cup and sometimes have underwiring for extra support – these are generally best for bigger-breasted women, while 'compression' bras press the breasts against the rib cage to reduce movement, and are well suited to flatter-chested women.

Choosing the right bra

- Comfort and fit come first. The bra should be snug but not so tight that it restricts your breathing. It should be level all the way round, not riding up at the back. Look for flat seams to avoid chafing.

- The straps should be wide enough to give proper support and not dig into your skin, but soft enough not to chafe. They should also be adjustable, since the fabric will stretch over time and you'll need to shorten them.

- As with all sports kit, cotton isn't ideal. Technical fabrics like Coolmax or Supplex wick away sweat so that your body stays dry and comfortable and you avoid chafing.

- If your breasts noticeably change size throughout your menstrual cycle, you may need to consider buying sports bras in different sizes to suit the time of the month.

- A crop top is not a sports bra. A study published in the *Journal of Science and Medicine in Sport* found that a crop top did not restrict breast movement as efficiently as a designated sports bra.

  See 'Further Information' for details of sports bra manufacturers and suppliers.

Autumn and winter running kit

Layering is the secret to comfortable winter running. Even when it's really cold outside, a bulky sweatshirt will feel heavy and stifling after a mile or two.

Bottom half

Running tights/tracksters: a much better option than heavy jogging bottoms, which will soon be stifling and sweat-soaked. Running tights or tracksters are designed for ease of movement and comfort as well as warmth.

OR

Thermal running tights: only necessary if you are running in extremely cold weather. Look for flat stitched seams, a reflective stripe for better visibility, and a pocket for keys or change. Ensure they are long enough, to prevent riding up.

Top half

A long-sleeved breathable top: this cold-weather essential is perfect on dry days under a gilet, and on chillier days it provides extra warmth under a thermal.

OR

Thermal top: to conserve heat and keep the wind off.

Waterproof jacket or gilet: go for a designated running waterproof, with such features as back vents, underarm splits, thumbholes to keep the sleeves down and reflective strips. One that packs away into itself, like a cagoule, is handy. A jacket with zip-off sleeves that can be made into a gilet is perfect, since it allows much more freedom of movement and isn't so heavy.

Hat: since we lose 50 per cent of our body heat through the head, a hat is a winter essential for running. A fleece or wool 'beanie' style works well.

Gloves: in cold temperatures, heat is shunted away from the extremities towards the internal organs. Lightweight fleece gloves or mittens will keep your hands warm while you run.

Top gear

Drinking vessel

It is worth investing in a designated running drinks bottle, which is easier to hold than a mineral water bottle. For longer training runs, especially those where you won't be passing any signs of civilization, you might consider a 'hydration system' (a backpack with a water bladder inside and a drinking tube that reaches round to your mouth). The smallest, lightest hydration solution of all is a £1 coin, with which you can buy your drink en route – and the change can be dispensed into a charity box.

Sunglasses

Sports sunglasses are a must if you are training in bright sunlight – prolonged exposure to UVA and UVB rays without eye protection can increase the risk of eye damage. Sport sunglasses are designed to stay on even when you are moving around a lot, and usually have a wraparound style and a sweat-resistant nosebridge to prevent slippage. There are two other advantages of sunglasses: first, they make a barrier between you and the rest of the world, helping to ease any feelings of self consciousness, and second, they prevent flies and dust getting in your eyes.

Heart rate monitors and sports watches

A heart rate monitor consists of an elasticated chest-strap that transmits heart rate data to a wristwatch. A basic model will tell you what your heart rate is at any given moment and how long you've been running, but there are far more advanced options available. If you would sooner do without the heart rate monitor, you will need some kind of timing device. A normal watch is fine, but a proper sports watch is better, since it has features such as a countdown timer, a 'split time' function to record laps, a backlighter and big, easy-to-press buttons for when you're on the move.

Backpacks and belts

Just any old backpack won't do if you are running with provisions. What you need is one that straps firmly to the body without chafing, and which has a vented, breathable padded back, so that you don't end up with a giant sweat patch on yours. Other useful features to look out for are side pockets for drinks bottles and flat-zipped compartments for keys and other jangly things. Bumbag-style 'fuel belts' hold a few small bottles, allowing you to distribute the weight of your fluid more evenly and also enabling you to grab one and drink easily without fumbling around.

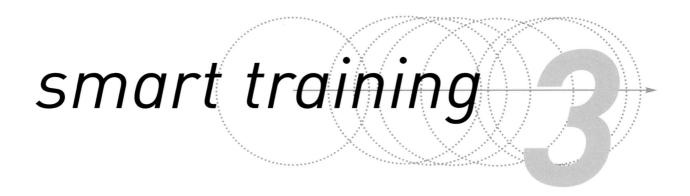

smart training

3

∴ Routine procedures

HOW, WHEN AND WHY TO WARM-UP, COOL DOWN AND STRETCH

In the previous chapter, we looked at the essential principles underpinning your training regime. This chapter deals with further aspects of the training itself. First, let's take a look at how to prepare for each run – warming up – and how to wind down after – cooling down and stretching.

The warm-up – why and how

A warm-up helps bridge the gap between stationary and 'in motion', allowing the body and mind time to respond and adapt to running. The warm-up has a number of functions: most importantly, it raises body temperature, increases heart rate, redirects blood flow away from the internal organs to the working muscles and mobilises the joints. Articular cartilage, which cushions the joint surfaces, does not have its own blood supply but relies on nutrients being delivered by synovial fluid, to reduce friction between the bone surfaces. Movement promotes the arrival of fresh fluid to soak the articular cartilage, as well as making it less 'sticky'.

Warming up not only makes running feel easier and more comfortable, but also makes it safer. A study

published in the *American Journal of Sports Medicine* found that a warmed-up muscle was less susceptible to injury than a cold one, while a study from the University of Strathclyde in Glasgow found that performing a warm-up reduced the accumulation of lactic acid in an all-out sprint.

Here are a few of the other benefits of a warm-up:

∴ Improved oxygen uptake by muscles, since haemoglobin, the oxygen-carrying molecule, releases its oxygen more readily at higher temperatures.

∴ Increased speed and efficiency of muscle contraction.

∴ Greater economy of movement.

∴ A reduced risk of muscle straining or tearing.

∴ A warm-up also helps to put you in the right mental state for a run – giving you time to focus your thoughts on the forthcoming session and put worries and daily stresses aside temporarily.

How to do it

Even though running is predominantly a lower-body activity, you don't want to start running with stiffness or tension in other areas, so gently mobilise the major joints of the body – the neck, shoulders, waist, hips, knees and ankles. All these movements should be very gentle, not vigorous swinging but controlled circling, bending and extending. Next, take a walk, either on the spot or forwards, gradually increasing your speed and range of movement to break into a slow jog.

Your warm-up should take at least five minutes – if you are doing a short, fast session or race, the warm-up should be longer and more thorough than if you are embarking on a slower, more prolonged run. This is partly because you don't want to spend precious minutes getting up to speed in a shorter session, but also because faster running and racing puts you at more risk of injury. Don't allow too much time to pass between completing the warm-up and beginning the activity – otherwise the benefits will be lost. See page 49 for a warm-up routine.

Should I stretch before I run?

Some running coaches and experts wouldn't dream of suggesting you run without stretching first, while others don't believe it necessary at all. Studies looking at the inclusion of stretching in a warm-up have not shown any clear benefit for its inclusion. A study looking at pre-exercise stretching for the prevention of injury in army recruits, published in the journal *Medicine and Science in Sports & Exercise*, found that it offered no additional injury prevention benefits over and above a standard warm-up. I guess it's a personal thing: if you feel the need to stretch, then your body probably needs to. But one thing's for sure: never stretch cold muscles – always warm-up first.

The cool-down – why and how

Once you've accomplished your run, it's tempting to leave it at that and get on with your day, but cooling down, or warming down, as it's sometimes called, is every bit as important as warming up. All it really means is coming to a gradual – rather than a sudden – stop. This prevents you from suffering undesirable effects such as dizziness, blood pooling in the veins and a sudden drop in blood pressure. It also prepares your body to return to a resting state, speeding up the removal of lactic acid from your muscles, reducing the likelihood of cramping or muscle spasm and possibly going some way towards preventing muscle stiffness and hastening recovery.

How to do it

All you need to do is slow down your running speed to a gentle jog, and then a walk. Maintain this until your breathing and heart rate have returned to normal. Then get ready to stretch. You can get showered and changed into something warm and comfortable before stretching – you don't need to do it the moment you walk in the door; 20 minutes or so won't allow the muscles to get too cold.

Staying flexible

Few subjects in running are as hotly debated as that of stretching. Does it improve performance, does it reduce injury risk, is it, indeed, worth doing at all? And if so – when? A major report in the *Journal Physician and Sportsmedicine* in 2000 assessed over 60 studies on stretching in order to make some general conclusions and recommendations. The authors pointed out that, while stretching is widely promoted as an integral component of any fitness programme, the evidence to back this up is decidedly scant and largely anecdotal. In fact, a study published in the *International Journal of Sports Medicine* in 2002 concluded that, among elite male distance runners, those with the least flexibility in the trunk and hamstrings had the greatest running economy. Meanwhile, Swedish research concluded that while stretching improved range of motion, this had no bearing on running performance, either negatively or positively.

While the debate rages on, we can do one of two things, wait for the science bods to make up their minds, or look at the current evidence and make our own decision.

Personally, I think flexibility work is important for anyone who sits down most of the day or does a repetitive job – and vital for runners. Christopher Norris, a physiotherapist and author of *The Complete Guide to Stretching*, points out that 'body tissues must be taken through their full range of motion to maintain their extensibility and elasticity. When this does not occur, the muscle can shorten permanently and alter the function of a joint.' While we can't categorically say that stretching will reduce injury risk or improve performance, it will help to restore muscles to their optimal length after the continual contraction involved in running, and it will help to maintain range of motion in the joints and prevent tightness and imbalances between muscle groups.

Using improved range of motion as their parameter of 'benefit', the researchers from the *Physician and Sportsmedicine* review concluded that a regime of regular static stretching, holding each stretch for 30 seconds, was advisable.

It's not known whether our physiological capacity for stretching improves over time, enabling us to stretch further, or whether, as recent research suggests, regular practice simply increases our stretch 'tolerance', in other words, our ability to hold a position without pain. Whichever is correct – these gains make it all the more likely that you'll continue to stretch – and who knows, maybe even enjoy it....

How to do it

Many runners are a law unto themselves when it comes to stretching practices, so don't just copy someone else's stretch routine – you may well be picking up inappropriate stretches and missing out on important ones. Always know what muscle or muscles you are stretching, and ensure you use good technique. The stretch routine on pages 50–5 is based on the static stretching protocol. This is the kind of stretching most of us are familiar with, in which you take the muscle to a point at which it feels tight and taut and hold the position. There are, of course, other ways to stretch; for example, active stretching, in which you contract one muscle to its fullest capacity in order to stretch the opposite (antagonistic) muscle to its greatest outer range, and proprioceptive neuromuscular facilitation (PNF), which sets out to 'trick' the stretch receptors into allowing the muscle to extend further. Some research suggests that PNF techniques offer marginally greater increases in range of motion compared to static stretching, but they do take a bit more effort and may increase the risk of injury.

Meanwhile, a study published in the *Journal of*

Orthopaedic Sports and Physical Therapy, found that continuous static stretching was superior to active stretching. So, for the purposes of marathon training, we'll stick to static stretching. This is a very safe and simple method, and good for post-workout, since it is relaxing and doesn't require you to do anything other than maintain the position.

How long? The *Physician and Sportsmedicine* study found that after six weeks, those who held a stretch for only 15 seconds gained far less range of movement than those who held each position for 30 seconds. Research also suggests that some muscle groups need to be held in stretch for longer than others, and that injured muscle tissue may need longer in order to increase range of motion. Flexibility varies from joint to joint – you may find your calves and hamstrings have an impressive range of motion while your lower back is as stiff as a board. Or that your right side is stiffer than your left. If this is the case, work harder on the tighter side, otherwise you'll simply maintain the imbalances.

How far? Stretch until you feel tension and a slight 'irritation' in the muscle but not pain. As the muscle relaxes, you can move slightly deeper into the stretch and hold again. Do not bounce in and out of your 'end' position unless you want your muscles to snap like overstretched elastic bands!

How often? After every run – particularly your long run and tougher sessions. In fact, if you can stretch daily, even better.

Warm-up exercises

These three warm-up exercises are especially good for runners, since they focus on the muscles and movement patterns that will be used during the running action.

1 Prone kicks

Prone kicks put your knee joints through a full range of motion without the impact of running – this helps to get the synovial fluid moving, protecting and feeding the joint cartilage. Lie face down with your forehead resting on your folded arms and your tummy gently pulled in. Bring one foot up towards the bottom and then take it back to the floor, simultaneously bringing the other foot up to the bottom. Start slowly and gradually speed up, kicking for 1–2 minutes or counting 120 kicks. Don't allow the pelvis to 'rock' from side to side.

2 Reverse walking

OK, so you aren't going to be running backwards, but as well as improving co-ordination this exercise activates the gluteal muscles, which are important in stabilising the pelvis during running. With each step, take the foot across the mid-line of the body (in other words, slightly across the front foot). Try 4–6 x 8 steps.

3 Hamstring swings

This exercise puts the hip through a full range of movement with no impact, and warms up the hamstrings. Stand side on to a support and, with knee bent, lift leg to hip height, and swing it up, down and back in a circular motion, with the leg almost fully extended at the end of the backswing. Do 10–20 on each leg, increasing the range and speed with each one but maintaining control throughout. Only do this after you have walked or jogged for a few minutes and have mobilised the joints.

Full body stretch for marathon runners

The routine on the following pages addresses all the muscles a runner needs to stretch. Perform it after every run if you can. Hold each position for 30 seconds (per side, if appropriate) and ideally, perform each stretch twice.

1

Hamstrings

Stand face on to a support between knee and hip height. Extend one leg and place it on the support, with the foot relaxed. Your supporting leg should be perpendicular to the floor. Now hinge forward from the hips (don't round your back), keeping the pelvis level and the knee of the extended leg straight. Feel the stretch along the back of the supported thigh. You don't need to pull your toes back towards you – the only reason this intensifies the stretch is because it adds the sciatic nerve into the equation.

2

Chest and shoulders

Stand in a split stance in an open doorway, with your arms at shoulder height and arms bent to 90 degrees. Lean into the doorway, not allowing shoulders to hunch up, and feel a stretch along the front of the chest and shoulders.

3

Quads

Stand tall with feet parallel and then lift your right heel, taking your right hand behind you to grab the foot. Bring the pelvis in to a neutral position and gently press the foot into your hand, keeping knees close together. It doesn't matter if your stretching thigh is in front of the supporting one, as long as you feel a stretch.

4 Upper and lower calves and feet

Stand facing a support, feet a stride length apart with back leg straight and front leg bent. Press the back heel into the floor so that you experience a stretch in the middle of the calf muscle (1). Turn toes slightly inwards to focus on the outer side of the calf. Hold. Now bring the back leg in a little, bend the knee and flex the hips, so that the stretch moves down to the lower part of the calf and Achilles tendon (2). Finally, with both legs still bent, place the toes of the back foot up against the heel of the front foot to stretch the muscles of the foot (3).

1

2

3

5 Inner thighs (adductors)

Sit on the floor with knees drawn into chest and feet flat on the floor. Drop knees open to the sides and use your elbows to gently press the legs open (1). Don't round the back; sit up tall. Hold, then extend the legs out to the sides and hinge forward from the hips (2).

1

2

51

6 *ITB/tensor fascia latae*
Stand tall, and cross one leg behind the other, sliding it away from you until you feel a stretch in the back leg hip. Bend the supporting leg and lean the torso in the direction the back leg is stretching.

7 *Hip flexors*
Assume a lunge position, allowing the back knee to go to the floor, and the toes to face down. Tighten the tummy muscles and extend forwards from the back hip, until your front knee is at 90 degrees. You should feel a stretch along the front of the back hip joint and thigh.

8 *Shins (tibialis anterior)*
Kneel on a mat with a rolled up towel under your feet. Gently lower your weight onto your haunches and feel a stretch along the front of the shins and ankles. To increase the stretch, place both hands on the floor, and lift each thigh alternately, 20 times in total.

9 Glutes/outer thighs (abductors)

Sit against a wall with legs outstretched. Cross your right foot over your left thigh and put the foot flat on the floor. Now take your left arm around the right knee and gently pull it around towards the shoulder (rather than hugging directly to chest), sitting up tall.

10 Hip rotators

Lie face up on the floor and bring one knee into your chest, the other leg flat on the floor. Now grasp the ankle of the bent leg and, stabilising the knee with your other hand, gently pull it across the body until you feel a deep hip stretch in the lifted leg.

11 Lower back

Roll onto your back, bend your knees in towards your chest and link your arms around them. Pull the knees towards the shoulders, pressing the lower back into the floor.

Stretched for time?

In an ideal world, we would all spend 15 minutes stretching after every run, but unfortunately, that isn't always a luxury we can afford. So if you are short on time, what are the crucial muscles to stretch? Focus on those that you usually find most tight, advises Sarah Connors, physiotherapist for UK Athletics, rather than just going for the obvious ones. A great three-in-one stretch, which targets muscle groups that often get short and tight through running, is the Thomas Test. This will stretch the hip flexors, the quads and iliotibial band. Using a bench or table, sit on the edge, pull one knee into your chest and roll backwards, allowing the other leg to hang over the table edge, completely relaxed, but in line with your torso (not dropping out to the side). To increase the stretch along the quads, gently draw your dangling foot towards the bench or table; to focus on the ITB, draw the stretching leg across the mid-line.

why we are here

Regular aerobic exercise helps you sleep better. A Stanford University study found that people who exercised for at least 40 minutes, four times a week, fell asleep twice as fast and woke up feeling more refreshed than non-exercisers.

{ *Rest up. It's crucial to incorporate rest into your schedule. You need at least one day a week of no vigorous exercise.*

Nerve stretches

Nerve stretching can help free up nerves that have become compressed or shortened as a result of bad posture or repeated poor movement patterns, and is particularly important after an injury, since it prevents swollen soft tissues sticking to the nerve and hampering neuromuscular pathways. But nerves should be treated carefully and not overstretched. Try these two nervous system stretches once or twice a week. The sensation should be of tightness and tingling rather than pins and needles and outright pain.

1

Sciatic nerve stretch
This is the most important nerve for runners to stretch. Lie on the floor with both legs out straight. Raise your right leg, bending at the knee and grasp your hands behind the knee. Slowly straighten the leg, keeping your knee directly above the hip and reaching the toes towards the body. 'Pulse' the foot towards the torso 20 times. Swap sides, and then repeat twice.

2

The slump
This stretches the whole of the nervous system. Sit on the edge of a table, link your arms behind your back and begin rolling forward through the spine, starting by taking the chin to the chest. Simultaneously straighten one leg, pulling the toes up towards you and locking the knee. Gently swing the leg 20 times. Perform on the other leg, and then repeat twice on both sides.

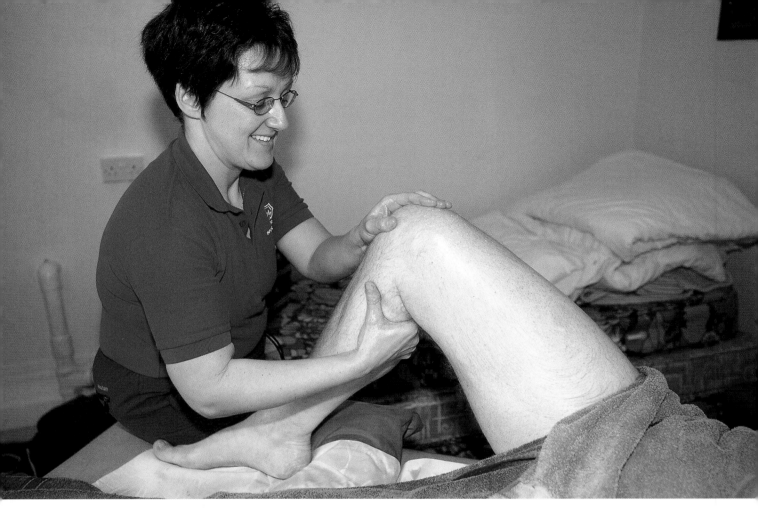

⫶ Body maintenance

HOW TO KEEP YOUR BODY BALANCED, INJURY-FREE AND IN GREAT SHAPE THROUGHOUT MARATHON TRAINING.

Our bodies may be designed to move, but they aren't necessarily designed to withstand regular, repetitive motion in a single direction, which is what they get with distance running. Perhaps that's why, in a typical year, nearly two-thirds of runners suffer an injury bad enough to put them out of action. Despite being fantastic exercise, running isn't an 'all-round' form of activity — it uses predominantly the lower body muscles, for a start, and it uses them in a very specific, repetitive way. The upshot is that some muscles (the running ones) are likely to get short and tight, while others (the non-running muscles) become weak. If you want to reduce the risk of injury and maintain a strong, healthy balanced body, it's important to complement your running with exercises that will balance out the equation. While it isn't possible to predict what might go wrong with everyone's individual body, there are some classic 'weak links' that catch out a significant number of budding marathoners every year.

Poor core stability

The basic idea of core stability is that if the abdominals and back, the body's core, are strong, they will protect the spine, enhance posture, minimise the risk of injury and improve sports technique and performance. Think of core stability as an 'internal corset' that keeps the pelvic girdle and spine in perfect position, and provides a stable base from which the body's limbs can move. Without it, the pelvis often 'tips' forward, compromising the ability of muscles that attach to it (such as the hip flexors and hamstrings) to work properly. In addition, the lower back arches and the tummy sticks out, leaving the spine vulnerable to injury and you looking like a duck on the run.

So what's the key to gaining core stability? It's not just a matter of cracking the whip – the problem is often as much to do with inefficient recruitment (the stabilising muscles have 'forgotten' what to do) as with strength. Exercises 1 to 4 in the workout on pages 69–70 will help get your core stabilisers functioning properly.

Pelvic instability and glute weakness

The muscles that stabilise the hip when the foot lands during running are the gluteals, particularly the gluteus medius and minimus, and the deep hip stabilisers: the piriformis and obturators. If these are weak (and they often are, since they spend so much time in a lengthened, unused position while we are seated), a muscle called the tensor fascia latae steps in to compensate. Since this attaches to the iliotibial band, it can cause the latter to become overtight or inflamed. If you aren't able to keep your pelvis stable and level when you lean back against a wall and lift each knee alternately up in front of you, try exercises 5 to 9.

Calf/shin imbalance

The calves work very hard during running, and develop quickly when you begin a running programme. If they develop too quickly, or become overstrong compared to their opposites, the tibialis anterior muscles along the front of the shin, you could end up with all manner of shin problems (commonly known as shin splints). Weak glute muscles can also cause the calves to overwork during running. Exercise 11 will help redress the balance, while exercises 5 to 9 will get the glutes working. The shin and calf stretches on page 51–2 are also essential.

Knee maltracking

If you've ever suffered from a sensation of 'heat' behind the kneecap or had 'runner's knee', it may be that your knee joint mechanics aren't up to scratch. The kneecap sits in a groove on the front of the thighbone, on which it slides up and down. If for some reason it is slightly off-kilter, it can cause irritation and inflammation under the kneecap. Often the reason for is that the kneecap is being pulled out of line by tight lateral structures at the outside of the knee joint, such as an overtight iliotibial band, or it may be that the innermost quad muscle, the vastus medialis obliquus (VMO), is too weak. A simple way to spot obvious knee maltracking is to simply stand in front of a mirror with your feet facing forwards, slightly apart. If the kneecap is tilted, or points left or right rather than straight head, it is indicative of maltracking. Try exercises 6 and 10.

The body maintenance workout

This is designed to do three things: improve your core stability, get your other stabilising muscles functioning properly and balance strength between muscle groups – honing your movement patterns, co-ordination and proprioception and reducing the likelihood of you being put out of action by an injury. You may choose to do all of the exercises, or just select those that seem most appropriate to you. An indication of how often to do each one, and how many to do is included.

Do I need to do these exercises if I already strength-train?

General strength training is fine for building general strength, but if you want specific strength for running, these exercises are better. The term 'functional strength' is used because the exercises use the muscles in the same way they would be used during running, or create better balance by recruiting muscles not used in the running gait cycle. See pages 64–5 for more on cross-training for strength.

The body maintenance exercises

1 Abdominal hollowing

Aim: to identify and strengthen the core stabilisers. Kneel on all fours with hands under shoulders and knees under hips. Allow your back to retain its natural curves and let your tummy 'hang' towards the floor. Now imagine you are doing up a zip from your pubic bone to belly button, sucking in the lower part of the tummy and simultaneously pulling up the pelvic floor while keeping your back perfectly still. Hold for 5 seconds, breathing freely and build up to 10 seconds.

2 x 10 before/after every run

2 Toe touchdowns

This is a more challenging core stability exercise. Lie on your back with knees bent and feet flat on the floor. Place one or both hands under your lower back (palms facing down) and contract your abdominals and pelvic floor until you feel your back press against the hands. Maintaining this pressure, slowly lift one foot a few inches off the floor, pause, then lower it. Now lift the other foot and continue to alternate until you lose the pressure against your hands. Don't be afraid to stop, 'regroup' and try again with this exercise!

2 x 12 2–3 times a week

3 Side bridge

Aim: to strengthen the lateral stabilisers in trunk. Lie on your side, supporting yourself on the elbow and front hand, with your legs stacked and body aligned. Keeping navel pulled to spine, raise up on to the elbow. Hold for 5 seconds, then release.

2 x 5 2–3 times a week

Running arms

Aim: to increase upper body strength and challenge core stability. Standing with good posture and navel to spine, move your arms in a full running motion arms on the spot, using dumbbells between 1 and 5 kg.

1 x 50 daily

Tip: even if you don't have weights to hand, it's worth doing this exercise providing you maintain core stability.

Hip hitch

Aim: to improve gluteal strength and pelvic stability. Stand sideways on a step, with your support leg bent at about 25 degrees and the other leg hanging over the edge. Now 'hitch' the hip, so that the pelvis becomes level. Hold for 2 seconds, then sink back down and repeat. Swap sides.

2 x 25 on each side before/after every run.

Wall ball squat

Aim: to hone hip and knee stability and strength. Lean on a fitball against the wall (or just the wall if necessary) – the ball level with your lower/mid back. Keeping navel to spine and knees directly above toes, slowly lower until your legs form a 90 degree angle at the knee (1). Pause, then straighten and repeat. Once you can do this comfortably, repeat the exercise with just one foot in contact with the floor – the other leg extended and raised in front (2).

3 x 10 2–3 times a week.

1
2

The bridge

Aim: to strengthen gluteals, lower back and adductors and improve pelvic stability. Lie on the floor with knees bent and feet flat, and a cushion between your knees. Raise the body up enough to allow the pelvis to clear the floor, squeezing the cushion with your inner thighs. Hold for 10 seconds, then release (1). Once you can do this comfortably, do the same as above, but once your pelvis is raised, alternately extend one leg and then the other, without allowing the pelvis to rock from side to side or the cushion to drop (2).

3 x 10 before/after every run

Hip opener

Aim: to strengthen the glute medius and deep hip rotators. Lie on your side, with pelvis square and hips and knees bent. Leaving the heels together, slowly lift the top knee by turning out at the hip but only go as far as you can without letting the pelvis or back twist. Hold for 2 seconds, then lower and repeat.

2 x 12 before/after every run

Supine leg lift

Aim: to strengthen the glutes and stretch tight hip flexors. Pull the belly button to spine and squeeze both buttocks to flatten the lower back. Bend one leg to a right angle, and raise it a couple of inches from the floor without rocking the pelvis (1). Hold for 5 seconds. Once you can do the full set without 'juddering' in the buttocks, perform with a straight leg extended (2). Swap sides.

1–2 x 10 2–3 times a week.

10 ### The squeeze
Aim: to strengthen the VMO, adductors and glutes. Sit on an upright chair with a cushion between your knees, your feet parallel. Squeeze the cushion for 10 seconds, contracting the glutes at the same time. Gradually release but don't let the cushion drop, and repeat.
1 x 10 daily

11 ### Toe curler
Aim: to improve lower leg muscle balance and strengthen lower leg and foot muscles. Stand on a stair barefoot, with toes extending over the edge. Bend the toes as if gripping the edge for a count of two, then flex them upwards and hold for two (1 & 2). Then turn around and with heels dropping over the edge of the step, rise up on to the toes and then drop slowly back down, keeping gluteals contracted (3 & 4).
2 x 10 toe lifts, 3 x 10 calf drops, 2–3 times a week

Eight more ways to reduce the risk of injury

 Rest up. It's crucial to incorporate rest into your schedule. You need at least one day a week of no vigorous exercise.

 Don't neglect your flexibility work, your warm-up or your cool-down. These aren't just pastimes for bored athletes but an essential part of your training.

 Don't allow niggles to go neglected. If anything hurts when you come back from your run, ice it for 10–15 minutes, either with an ice pack or using ice massage (see page 115). This can help reduce inflammation and prevent the problem continuing. If it still hurts, don't run on it, but rest and if necessary see a sports medicine expert.

 Don't overdo things. The number one reason for injuries, according to sports physiotherapist Alan Watson, is doing too much, too quickly, not poor biomechanics.

 Free up your knees. Watson recommends 'patella mobilisations' for all marathon runners. These help to prevent tight structures causing the kneecap to get misaligned and you can do them in front of the TV or at work. With your leg straight out in front of you but relaxed, move the kneecap medially, laterally and diagonally in a firm, repetitive pulsing motion. (A tea towel can help you get a good grip.) Then bend the leg a little and push the kneecap directly down. You'll need to do at least 50 in each direction.

 Get a rubdown. While numerous studies insist there is no proof of the benefits of sports massage, the fact that nearly all elite athletes consider it to be an important part of their regime cannot be ignored. Sports massage involves specific techniques and is a very deep tissue massage, which encourages fresh supplies of oxygenated blood to reach the muscle tissues and flush out metabolic waste products and toxins. More importantly, perhaps, it frees up the collagen fibres around each muscle sheath, and prevents 'sticking'. In a recent study published in the *British Journal of Sports Medicine*, researchers found that a massage given two hours after exercise reduced the intensity of soreness 48 hours later, although it did not improve function in the muscles that had been working. It also feels good, which is an important factor in staying motivated.

 Consider taking glucosamine sulphate supplements. Read more on this on page 108.

 Be 'body aware' all the time, not just when you are running. There's no use in hunching over your computer all day, or slumping in front of the TV in the evening, only to then try to perfect your posture when you are running. Good posture – including core stability – is something you should strive for 24 hours a day.

Cross-training – or straining?

Most runners have heard of cross-training – the notion of mixing other activities into your weekly regime to complement your running. Going back to those principles of training, remember 'specificity'? The idea that to get better at distance running, you have to run long distances. Well, in a way cross-training flies in the face of specificity, because it suggests that taking part in other activities will improve your performance in your main activity (that would be marathon running for you).

So what does the evidence say? Researchers at California State University looked at five weeks of mixed cycling and running (alternate days) compared to a running-only programme of equal intensity. After five weeks, both groups had maintained aerobic performance, suggesting that cross-training could be of benefit. Another study, published in the journal *Medicine and Science in Sport & Exercise*, looked at the effects of cross-training versus running for six weeks on 5 km run time and found similar improvements in both subject groups. These results support the use of cycling as a form of cross-training to maintain running fitness, but remember, it didn't improve performance over and above running alone, which begs the question – why not stick to running?

The role and value of cross-training have a lot to do with what you expect to get out of it. Is it a way of getting cardiovascular exercise without the impact of running? Is it a way of balancing your programme by using muscles that running doesn't use? Is it a mental break as much as a physical one? Is it a strategy to keep training while injured? These questions determine whether cross-training is appropriate and if so, what type. A long-term research project from Johns Hopkins University looked at professional female swimmers over a seven-year period and found that as many injuries were sustained in cross-training activities as were caused by swimming. This demonstrates that engaging in activities you aren't used to needs to be done with caution.

However, there are times when cross-training is useful, and even essential. Your heart and lungs may get a fantastic aerobic workout if you go out cycling and aren't accustomed to it. Even though you aren't pounding the streets – they can't tell the difference. But you do need to make running your main activity in order to allow to musculoskeletal system to adapt to the demands of running.

Cross-training for aerobic fitness

For those new to running, mixing in non-impact activities may help protect you from injury while still giving you sufficient cardiovascular exercise to get round the marathon course. Alan Watson recommends the cross-trainer (elliptical trainer) and the stepper in preference to the bike or swimming as aerobic activities, because they use the running muscles in the same kind of way. Recent research has shown that the elliptical trainer offers a comparable workout to running. However, while calorie burn was similar in both activities, the exercisers in the study felt they were working harder on the elliptical trainer, possibly because they weren't used to it. If you choose to take the impact off your joints by cross-training on the elliptical, try not to hold on to the handles as soon as you are accustomed to the machine. Use your arms in a 'running' motion to closer mimic your sport.

Other aerobic cross-training options

- Cycling helps improve aerobic endurance, without impact on joints.
- Swimming improves ankle flexibility, upper body strength, and allows hip flexors to lengthen.
- The Stairclimber is a good substitute for hill work.

Cross-training for strength

Do endurance athletes need to lift weights to improve performance? Sarah Connors, a physiotherapist for UK Athletics, believes that as far as running is concerned, the further you go, the less you need to lift weights. To understand why, you need to know a little about muscle fibre types.

There are two principal types of muscle fibre in the body – we all have some of both, but the type that predominates varies from person to person, and the intensity and duration of an activity determines what fibre type is preferentially recruited. Endurance athletes tend to have a lot of 'slow-twitch' or type 1 fibres (muscle biopsies on marathon runners have revealed as much as 70 per cent slow-twitch fibres). These fibres are highly resistant to fatigue, but tend to be recruited mainly at low intensities. Fast-twitch fibres (type 2), on the other hand, are associated with muscle power, strength and speed – and are recruited at very high intensities.

However, there are two types of type 2 fibres – type 2a and type 2b. While 2b are the hardcore high-intensity sort, the type 2a fibres are more middle-of-the-road, and, depending on the type of training you do, can be made to act more like type 1 or type 2b fibres. Endurance training will make them be type 1 'wannabes', while the wrong type of resistance training – hard efforts of lifting weights over a short period of time – is likely to make your type 2a fibres more like 2b fibres.

If you want to strength train over and above the 'body maintenance workout' set out above, then go for a moderate weight and low volume – say one set instead of three. That way, you'll gain what is known as 'muscular endurance', as well as benefiting from stronger connective tissues (ligaments and tendons), increased calorie expenditure (due to higher muscle mass) and use of the muscles that don't get used in running. Researchers from the University of Maryland got volunteer novice exercisers to cycle to exhaustion and recorded their times. They then put them on a thrice-weekly strength training pro-gramme for 12 weeks. At the end of the period, leg strength had increased significantly (as might be expected) but cycle time had also increased, by 33 per cent.

Cross-training as a necessity

Sometimes cross-training isn't just for fun or variety – it's a necessity. If you are injured, and unable to withstand the high forces of running, or are returning from an injury and need to proceed with caution, cross-training is a useful tool for maintaining – or at least minimising – the loss of fitness. For runners, one of the best ways of doing this is water-running. It's perfect, since the mechanics are barely different from running on land, and research has shown that it can be as aerobically challenging, partly because water has 12 times the resistance of air. You can perform water-running with or without a buoyancy belt (it's harder without). This device is secured around your hips so you don't have to work so hard not to sink. If you're giving water-running a try, bear the following tips in mind:

- The water must be deep enough for you to move your legs without touching the bottom of the pool.

- Remember to use your arms in a running motion rather than paddling.

- Try to hit the pool off-peak – not only to avoid curious onlookers, but so that you get the space you need to train.

- Aim for a leg turnover of roughly half your land leg turnover speed.

- Don't lean forwards – stay upright.

- Don't be afraid to take breaks on your first few attempts – this is tough training, so go for 3 to 5 minute bouts with a 30 second recovery in between – 15 to 20 minutes total is sufficient to start with.

- Mimic your running sessions, rather than paddling monotonously for the same time and at the same speed every visit.

why we are here

Running might increase your body's production of 'free radicals', but it also enhances your body's ability to soak them up and its ability to cope with these potentially harmful chemicals, says the American College of Sports Medicine.

⫶ 16 weeks to success

JOHN BREWER'S 16-WEEK PROGRAMME FOR THREE LEVELS OF COMMITMENT –
TO SUIT ALL LEVELS OF INEXPERIENCE!

You've read the theory, bought the kit, and you are raring to go! This is where you will find the core 16-week training schedules that underpin this book. Each of the three programmes offers a slightly different approach to marathon training, and within each, there are two levels – you can decide which level to follow by using your score from the 'fitness assessments' described on page 5–6.

The first training programme is the 'Ideal World', for those with the time and commitment to really train properly. It contains plenty of variety, and a steady build-up, in terms of distance, as the weeks progress. If you can follow this at either level, from start to finish, you will have prepared well and stand a good chance of completing the 26.2 miles in a time to be proud of.

The second programme, which is called 'Real World', is for runners with less time – or inclination – to give to marathon training. As with the Ideal World programme, there is a steady build-up in intensity and duration as the weeks progress, although the total distance covered at both Level 1 and Level 2 is less.

The third programme isn't called 'Bare Minimum' for nothing. This is geared towards the time-crunched runner, and really is just about the least amount of training you could get away with and still expect to get around the 26.2-mile course. You'll still need to focus on some high quality training at week-ends, although the weekday runs are less time consuming and based around shorter, maintenance sessions.

Before you decide whether you are training in the ideal world, the real world or with the bare minimum of effort, bear in mind that the real beauty of these programmes is that they have been designed to be interchangeable. You can move from one to another, so long as you stick to the appropriate week. So, for example, you have done five weeks in the Ideal World, and suddenly hit a busy patch at work: you can switch to the Real World for a fortnight, or even permanently. Similarly, if you are following a Level 1 programme, and are finding it too easy, you can switch to Level 2 either on the same, or a different, programme. This flexible approach should help accommodate your needs, and provide the progression and variety that a good marathon training programme makes.

Days of the week for each run are not specified – it is up to you to fit the runs in when suits you best, but try to follow tougher sessions with rest days, and space the runs out throughout the week.

If you have to miss a session – or even more than one – try to maintain the long run and a swifter session, such as the threshold run or longer intervals. Remember, you can always 'walk-run' the long runs if you find the distances challenging. A good rule of thumb is to run for 8 min and walk for 2, or run for 9 min and walk for 1 – it's also easy to keep track of on your sports watch.

Finally, you will see that all three programmes follow a '3 weeks hard, 1 week light' philosophy. This means that after each three-week period of hard training, there is a fourth week where the overall volume of training is reduced, and some cross-training is introduced. This gives the body a chance to adapt to the physiological overload it has been experiencing, as well as re-charging your physical and mental batteries before the next three weeks of training. Ready to get started?

ideal world training programme level 1

1

1   *Steady run:* 20 mins Effort 2
2   *Hill :* 25 mins Effort 2 – with 4 x 1 min hills at Effort 3, jogging back to recover
3   *Steady run:* 20 mins Effort 2
4   *Long run:* 5–6 miles Effort 1

2

1   *Hills:* 20 mins Effort 2 – with 5 x 30 second hills at Effort 4, jogging back to recover
2   *Easy run:* 30 mins Effort 1
3   *Fartlek:* 25 mins – to include 6 x 30 second bursts at Effort 4
4   *Long run:* 6–7 miles Effort 1

3

1   *Threshold run:* 20 mins Effort 3
2   *Fartlek:* 30 mins – to include 8 x 30 second bursts at Effort 4
3   *Steady run:* 30 mins Effort 2
4   *Long run:* 7–8 miles Effort 2

4

1   *Cross-training:* 30 mins
2   *Fartlek:* 25 mins inc. 8 x 30 seconds bursts at Effort 4
3   *Long run:* 8–9 miles Effort 1 OR 10km race

5

1   *Threshold run:* 20 mins Effort 3
2   *Hilly run:* 30 mins Effort 3 up hills, Effort 2 on downhill and flat
3   *Interval run:* 25 mins inc. 5 x 2 mins at Effort 4 with 2 min recovery at Effort 1
4   *Easy run:* 30 mins Effort 1
5   *Long run:* 9–10 miles Effort 1–2

6

1   *Interval run:* 30 mins inc. 4 x 3 min at Effort 4 with 3 min recoveries at Effort 1
2   *Threshold run:* 25 mins Effort 3
3   *Easy run:* 30 mins Effort 1
4   *Steady run:* 30 mins Effort 2
5   *Long run:* 10–11 miles Effort 2 OR 10 mile race (NB: Don't race today if you did a 10km in week 4)

7

1   *Steady run:* 35 mins Effort 2
2   *Interval run:* 45 mins inc. 4 x 4 mins at Effort 4, with 4 min recoveries at Effort 1, followed by 10 mins at Effort 3
3   *Steady run:* 50 mins Effort 2
4   *Threshold run:* 25 mins Effort 3
5   *Long run:* 12–13 miles Effort 2

8	1	**Easy run:** 40 mins Effort 1
	2	**Cross-training:** 30 mins
	3	**Steady run:** 1 hr Effort 2
	4	**Long run:** 13–14 miles Effort 1

9	1	**Speed session:** 30 mins inc. 5 x 60 seconds at Effort 4 with 60 second recoveries at Effort 1, followed by 5 mins at Effort 2 and then repeat
	2	**Steady run:** 1 hr Effort 2
	3	**Fartlek:** 50 mins of your choice
	4	**Interval run:** 30 mins inc. 5 x 3 mins at Effort 4, with 3 min recoveries at Effort 1
	5	**Long run:** 14–15 miles Effort 2

10	1	**Steady run:** 1 hr Effort 2
	2	**Threshold run:** 30 mins Effort 3
	3	**Hilly run:** 50 mins Effort 2 with 8 x 100m hills at Effort 4.
	4	**Interval run:** 25 mins, inc. 6 x 2 mins at Effort 4 with 2 min recoveries at Effort 1
	5	**Long run:** 15–16 miles Effort 2 OR Half Marathon Race

11	1	**Speed session:** 35 mins inc. 5 x 60 seconds at Effort 4 with 60 second recoveries at Effort 1, followed by 5 mins at Effort 2 and then repeat. Follow with 5 mins at Effort 3
	2	**Steady run:** 30 mins Effort 2
	3	**Fartlek run:** 40 mins to include 6 bursts of 30–60 seconds at Effort 4
	4	**Threshold run:** 25 mins Effort 3
	5	**Long run:** 17–18 miles Effort 2

12	1	**Easy run:** 1hr Effort 1
	2	**Cross-training:** 30 mins
	3	**Steady run:** 40 mins Effort 2
	4	**Long run:** 18–19 miles Effort 1

13	1	**Threshold Run:** 25 mins Effort 3
	2	**Steady run:** 45 mins Effort 2
	3	**Fartlek run:** 45 mins, to include 8 x 40–60 seconds at Effort 4 and last 10 mins at Effort 3
	4	**Long run:** 20–21 miles Effort 2

14	1	**Easy run:** 30 mins Effort 1
	2	**Interval run:** 20 mins inc. 4 x 2 mins at Effort 3 with 2 min recoveries at Effort 1
	3	**Threshold run:** 20 mins, Effort 3
	4	**Long run:** 10–11 miles Effort 1

15	1	**Interval run:** 20 mins inc. 5 x 1 min at Effort 3 with 1 min recoveries at Effort 1
	2	**Easy run:** 30 mins Effort 1 with last 10 mins at Effort 3
	3	**Cross-training:** 30 mins
	4	**Long run:** 5 miles Effort 2

16	1	**Easy run:** 30 mins Effort 1 with 5 20m strides at the end
	2	**Cross-training:** 30 mins OR Rest
	3	**Easy run:** 20–30 mins Effort 1 with 5x 20m strides at the end
	4	**Race Day**

ideal world training programme level 2

1
1. *Steady run:* 20 mins Effort 2
2. *Hill:* 25 mins Effort 2 – with 6 x 1 min hills at Effort 3, jogging back to recover
3. *Steady run:* 30 mins Effort 2
4. *Long run:* 5–6 miles Effort 2

2
1. *Hills:* 25 mins Effort 2 – with 6 x 30 second hills at Effort 4, jogging back to recover
2. *Easy run:* 40 mins Effort 1
3. *Fartlek:* 25 mins – to include 6 x 30 second bursts at Effort 4
4. *Long run:* 6–7 miles Effort 1

3
1. *Threshold run:* 20 mins Effort 3
2. *Fartlek:* 30 mins – to include 8 x 40 second bursts at Effort 4
3. *Steady run:* 35 mins Effort 2
4. *Long run:* 7–8 miles Effort 2

4
1. *Cross-training:* 40 mins
2. *Fartlek:* 30 mins inc. 8 x 40 seconds bursts at Effort 4
3. *Long run:* 8–9 miles Effort 1 OR 10km race

5
1. *Threshold run:* 25 mins Effort 3
2. *Hilly run:* 30 mins Effort 3 up hills, Effort 2 on downhill and flat
3. *Interval run:* 30 mins inc. 6 x 2 mins at Effort 4 with 2 min recovery at Effort 1
4. *Easy run:* 30 mins Effort 1
5. *Long run:* 10–11 miles Effort 1–2

6
1. *Interval run:* 40 mins inc. 5 x 3 min at Effort 4 with 3 min recoveries at Effort 1
2. *Threshold run:* 25 mins Effort 3
3. *Easy run:* 40 mins Effort 1
4. *Hilly run:* 30 mins Effort 3 up hills, Effort 2 on downhill and flat
5. *Long run:* 11–12 miles Effort 2 OR 10 mile race (NB: Don't race today if you did a 10km in week 4)

7
1. *Steady run:* 40 mins Effort 2
2. *Interval run:* 50 mins inc. 4 x 5 mins at Effort 4, with 5 min recoveries at Effort 1, followed by 10 mins at Effort 3
3. *Steady run:* 1 hr Effort 2
4. *Threshold run:* 30 mins Effort 3
5. *Long run:* 12–13 miles Effort 2

8
1 *Easy run:* 45 mins Effort 1
2 *Cross-training:* 40 mins
3 *Steady run:* 1 hr Effort 2
4 *Long run:* 13–14 miles Effort 2

9
1 *Speed session:* 30 mins inc. 5 x 60 seconds at Effort 4 with 60 second recoveries at Effort 1, followed by 5 mins at Effort 2 and then repeat
2 *Steady run:* 1 hr 15 mins Effort 2
3 *Fartlek:* 50 mins of your choice
4 *Interval run:* 40 mins inc. 10 x 2 mins at Effort 4, with 2 min recoveries at Effort 1
5 *Long run:* 14–15 miles Effort 2

10
1 *Steady run:* 1 hr 10 Effort 2
2 *Threshold run:* 30 mins Effort 3
3 *Hilly run:* 50 mins: 10 mins at Effort 2, then 10 x 100m hills at Effort 4
4 *Interval run:* 35 mins, inc. 8 x 2 mins at Effort 4 with 2 min recoveries at Effort 1
5 *Long run:* 15–16 miles Effort 2 OR Half Marathon Race

11
1 *Speed session:* 40 mins inc. 5 x 60 seconds at Effort 4 with 60 second recoveries at Effort 1, followed by 5 mins at Effort 2 and then repeat. Follow with 10 mins at Effort 3
2 *Steady run:* 30 mins Effort 2
3 *Fartlek run:* 40 mins to include 8 bursts of 30–60 seconds at Effort 4
4 *Threshold run:* 25 mins Effort 3
5 *Long run:* 17–18 miles Effort 1

12
1 *Easy run:* 1hr Effort 1
2 *Cross-training:* 40 mins
3 *Steady run:* 40 mins Effort 2
4 *Long run:* 19–20 miles Effort 2

13
1 *Threshold Run:* 25 mins Effort 3
2 *Steady run:* 50 mins Effort 2
3 *Fartlek run:* 50 mins, to include 10 x 40–60 seconds at Effort 4 and last 10 mins at Effort 3
4 *Long run:* 20–22 miles at Effort 2

14
1 *Easy run:* 30 mins Effort 1
2 *Interval run:* 30 mins inc. 5 x 2 mins at Effort 3 with 2 min recoveries at Effort 1
3 *Threshold run:* 25 mins, Effort 3
4 *Steady run:* 30 mins Effort 2
5 *Long run:* 10–11 miles Effort 2

15
1 *Interval run:* 30 mins inc. 5 x 1 min at Effort 3 with 1 min recoveries at Effort 1
2 *Easy run:* 30 mins Effort 1 with last 10 mins at Effort 3
3 *Steady run:* 30 mins Effort 2
4 *Long run:* 5 miles Effort 2

16
1 *Easy run:* 40 mins Effort 1 with 5 20m strides at the end
2 *Cross-training:* 30 mins OR Rest
3 *Easy run:* 20–30 mins Effort 1 with 5 20m strides at the end
4 *Race Day*

real world training programme level 1

1
1. *Easy run:* 25 mins Effort 1
2. *Hill :* 25 mins Effort 2 including 4 x 1 min hills at Effort 3: jogging back to recover
3. *Long run:* 4–5 miles Effort 2

2
1. *Hill run:* 20 mins Effort 2 including 5 x 1 min hills at Effort 3: jogging back to recover
2. *Fartlek run:* 30 mins including 6 x 30 seconds at Effort 4
3. *Long run:* 5–6 miles Effort 2

3
1. *Threshold run:* 20 mins Effort 3
2. *Fartlek run:* 30 mins – including 8 x 30 seconds at Effort 4
3. *Steady run:* 20 mins Effort 2
4. *Long run:* 6–7 miles Effort 1

4
1. *Cross-training:* 30 mins
2. *Fartlek run:* 25 mins including 3 x 1 min fast and 3 x hill climbs lasting 1 min, both at Effort 4
3. *Long run:* 7–8 miles Effort 2

5
1. *Threshold run:* 20 mins Effort 3
2. *Interval run:* 25 mins including 4 x 3 min at Effort 4 with 3 min recoveries at Effort 1
3. *Easy run:* 30 mins Effort 1
4. *Long run:* 8–9 miles Effort 2

6
1. *Interval run:* 30 mins 4 x 3 min faster bursts at Effort 4 with 3 min recoveries at Effort 1
2. *Easy run:* 40 mins Effort 1
3. *Hill run:* 30 mins: increasing speed to Effort 4 up hills: recovering downhill and on flat
4. *Long run:* 9–10 miles Effort 1 OR 10 km race

7
1. *Interval run:* 40 mins 4 x 4 min at Effort 4 with 4 min recoveries at Effort 1 – followed by 5 mins at Effort 3
2. *Threshold run:* 25 mins Effort 3
3. *Steady run:* 30 mins Effort 2
4. *Long run:* 10–11 miles Effort 2

8

1. **Easy run:** 40 mins Effort 1
2. **Cross-training:** 30 mins
3. **Long run:** 12–13 miles Effort 1

9

1. **Speed session:** 30 mins: 5 x 60 seconds Effort 4 with 60 second jog recovery: followed by 5 min jog and repeat
2. **Threshold run:** 30 mins Effort 3
3. **Steady run:** 1 hr Effort 2
4. **Long run:** 13–14 miles Effort 2

10

1. **Easy run:** 45 mins Effort 1
2. **Interval run: 30 mins:** to include 7 x 2 mins at Effort 4 with 2 min recoveries at Effort 1
3. **Long run:** 14–15 miles Effort 2 OR marathon race

11

1. **Speed session:** 30 mins: 5 x 60 seconds Effort 4 with 60 second jog recovery: followed by 5 min jog and repeat
2. **Steady run:** 30 mins Effort 2
3. **Threshold run:** 30 mins Effort 3
4. **Long run:** 16–17 miles Effort 1

12

1. **Easy run:** 1hr Effort 1
2. **Cross-training:** 30 mins
3. **Long run:** 17–18 miles Effort 2

13

1. **Threshold Run:** 30 mins Effort 3
2. **Steady run:** 45 mins at Effort 2
3. **Fartlek run:** 45 mins: to include 10 x 40–60 seconds at Effort 4 and last 10 mins at Effort 3
4. **Long run:** 19–20 miles Effort 2

14

1. **Easy run:** 30 mins Effort 1
2. **Interval run:** 20 mins including 4 x 2 mins at Effort 3 with 2 min recoveries at Effort 1
3. **Steady run:** 30 mins effort 2
4. **Long run:** 10–11 miles Effort 1

15

1. **Interval run:** 20 mins to include 4 x 1 min at Effort 3 with 1 min recoveries at Effort 1
2. **Easy run:** 40 mins Effort 1 with last 10 mins at Effort 3
3. **Long run:** 5 miles Effort 2

16

1. **Slow run:** 20 mins Effort 1 with 5x 20m strides at the end
2. **Cross-training:** 30 minutes OR **Slow run:** 20 mins Effort 1 with 5x 20m strides at the end
3. **Race Day**

real world
training programme
level 2

1
1	*Steady run:* 30 mins Effort 2
2	*Hill sission:* 25 mins Effort 2 including 6 x 1 min hills at Effort 3: jogging back to recover
3	*Long run:* 5–6 miles Effort 2

2
1	*Hill run:* 20 mins Effort 2 including 8 x 1 min hills at Effort 3: jogging back to recover
2	*Fartlek run:* 30 mins including 8 x 30 seconds at Effort 4
3	*Long run:* 6–7 miles Effort 2

3
1	*Threshold run:* 20 mins Effort 3
2	*Fartlek run:* 30 mins – including 8 x 40 seconds at Effort 4
3	*Steady run:* 30 mins Effort 2
4	*Long run:* 7–8 miles Effort 1

4
1	*Cross-training:* 40 mins
2	*Fartlek run:* 30 mins including 5 x 1 min fast and 5 x hill climbs at Effort 4
3	*Long run:* 7–8 miles Effort 2

5
1	*Threshold run:* 25 mins Effort 3
2	*Interval run:* 30 mins including 5 x 3 min at Effort 4 with 2 min recoveries at Effort 1
3	*Easy run:* 30 mins Effort 1
4	*Long run:* 9–10 miles Effort 2 OR 10 km race

6
1	*Interval run:* 30 mins 6 x 3 min faster bursts at Effort 4 with 3 min recoveries at Effort 1
2	*Hill run:* 30 mins: increasing speed to Effort 4 up hills: recovering downhill and on flat
3	*Long run:* 9–10 miles Effort 1 OR 10km race

7
1	*Interval run:* 40 mins 5 x 3 min at Effort 4 with 3 min recoveries at Effort 1 – followed by 10 mins at Effort 3
2	*Threshold run:* 30 mins Effort 3
3	*Steady run:* 40 mins Effort 2
4	*Long run:* 11–12 miles Effort 2

8

1   *Easy run:* 45 mins Effort 1
2   *Cross training:* 30 minutes
3   *Long run:* 13–14 miles Effort 1

9

1   *Speed session:* 30 mins: 5 x 60 seconds Effort 4 with 60 second jog recovery: followed by 5 min jog and repeat
2   *Threshold run:* 30 mins Effort 3
3   *Steady run:* 45 minutes Effort 2
4   *Long run:* 14–15 miles Effort 2

10

1   *Steady run:* 1 hr Effort 2
2   *Threshold split run:* 30 minutes – 7 minutes at Effort 3–4, 3 minute jog at Effort 1 x 3 repeats
3   *Interval run:* 30 mins: to include 7 x 2 mins at Effort 4 with 2 min recoveries at Effort 1
4   *Long run:* 15–16 miles Effort 2 OR marathon race

11

1   *Speed session:* 35 mins: 6 x 60 seconds Effort 4 with 60 second jog recovery: followed by 5 min jog and repeat
2   *Steady run:* 40 mins Effort 2
3   *Fartlek run:* 45 minutes Effort 2 with 10 mins at Effort 3 and 5 mins at Effort 4
4   *Long run:* 17–18 miles Effort 2

12

1   *Easy run:* 1hr Effort 1 with last 5 minutes at Effort 4
2   *Cross-training:* 40 mins
3   *Long run:* 19–20 miles Effort 1

13

1   *Threshold Run:* 30 mins Effort 3
2   *Steady run:* 45 mins at Effort 2
3   *Fartlek run:* 50 mins: to include 10 x 40–60 seconds at Effort 4 and last 10 mins at Effort 3
4   *Long run:* 20–22 miles Effort 2

14

1   *Easy run:* 45 mins Effort 1
2   *Interval run:* 25 mins including 5 x 2 mins at Effort 3 with 2 min recoveries at Effort 1
3   *Steady run:* 30 mins Effort 2
4   *Long run:* 10–11 miles Effort 2

15

1   *Interval run:* 20 mins to include 4 x 1 min at Effort 3 with 1 min recoveries at Effort 1
2   *Easy run:* 45 mins Effort 1 with last 10 mins at Effort 3
3   *Long run:* 5 miles Effort 2

16

1   *Easy run:* 20 mins Effort 1 with 5x 20m strides at the end
2   *Easy run:* 20 mins Effort 1 with 5x 20m strides at the end
3   *Race Day*

bare minimum training programme level

1
1. *Steady run:* 20 mins Effort 2
2. *Hill :* 20 mins at Effort 2 – with 5 x 1 min hills at Effort 3, jogging back to recover
3. *Long run:* 5–6 miles Effort 1

2
1. *Steady run:* 25 mins, Effort 2
2. *Fartlek run:* 30 mins – to include 8 x 30 seconds at Effort 3 and 4 x 1-min hill climbs at Effort 3
3. *Long run:* 6–7 miles Effort 1

3
1. *Threshold run:* 20 mins Effort 3
2. *Fartlek run:* 30 mins – include 10 x 30 seconds at Effort 4
3. *Steady run:* 35 mins Effort 2
4. *Long run:* 7–8 miles Effort 2

4
1. *Cross-training:* 30 mins
2. *Hill session:* 30 mins at Effort 2 – with 8 x 1 min hills at Effort 3, jogging back to recover
3. *Long run:* 8–9 miles, Effort 1

5
1. *Threshold run:* 25 mins Effort 3
2. *Interval run:* 35 mins including 5 x 3 min at Effort 4, with 2 min recoveries at Effort 1 and 10 mins at Effort 3 to finish
3. *Long run:* 9–10 miles Effort 2

6
1. *Steady run:* 40 mins Effort 2
2. *Hilly run:* 40 mins, increasing speed to Effort 4 up hills, recovering downhill and on flat
3. *Long run:* 10–11 miles Effort 1 OR 6–9 mile race

7
1. *Interval run:* 40 mins 5 x 3 mins at Effort 4, with 3 min recoveries at Effort 1, followed by 10 mins at Effort 3
2. *Threshold run:* 25 mins Effort 3
3. *Steady run:* 40 mins Effort 2
4. *Long run:* 11–12 miles Effort 2

8
1. *Interval run:* 35 mins 5 x 3 mins at Effort 4, with 2 mins jogging between, followed by 10 mins at Effort 3
2. *Long run:* 13–14 miles Effort 1

9
1. *Threshold run:* 30 mins Effort 3
2. *Easy run:* 40 mins Effort 1
3. *Speed session:* 30 mins: 5 x 1 min at Effort 4 with 1-min recovery at Effort 1. Five min jog, then repeat
4. *Long run:* 14–15 miles Effort 2

10
1. *Steady run:* 1 hr Effort 2
2. *Hill run:* 30 mins, to include 7 x 2 mins at Effort 4, with 2 min recoveries at Effort 1
3. *Long run:* 16–17 miles Effort 1 OR marathon race

11
1. *Speed session:* 20 mins: 8 x 60 seconds at Effort 4 with 60 second jog recovery, followed by 5 mins at Effort 2
2. *Threshold run:* 30 mins Effort 3
3. *Easy run:* 45 mins, Effort 1
4. *Long run:* 17–18 miles Effort 2

12
1. *Steady run:* 1hr Effort 2
2. *Split Threshold Run:* 8 mins at Effort 3, 2 mins jog x 4

13
1. *Steady run:* 40 mins Effort 2
2. *Fartlek run:* 45 mins, to include 10 faster bursts of 40–60 seconds at Effort 5 and last 10 mins at Effort 3
3. *Threshold run:* 25 mins Effort 3
4. *Long run:* 19–20 miles Effort 2

14
1. *Steady run:* 30 mins Effort 2
2. *Interval run:* 20 mins to include 4 x 2 mins Effort 4 with 2 mins recovery at Effort 1
3. *Long run:* 10 miles Effort 1

15
1. *Threshold run:* 30 mins Effort 3
2. *Easy run:* 40 mins Effort 1 with last 10 mins at Effort 3
3. *Long run:* 5 miles Effort 2

16
1. *Easy run:* 20 mins Effort 1 with 5x 20m strides at the end
2. *Easy run:* 20 mins OR *Cross-training:* 20 mins
3. *Race Day*

bare minimum training programme level 2

1
1. *Steady run:* 25 mins Effort 2
2. *Hill :* 20 mins at Effort 2 – with 6 x 1 min hills at Effort 3, jogging back to recover
3. *Long run:* 5–6 miles Effort 1

2
1. *Steady run:* 30 mins, Effort 2
2. *Fartlek run:* 30 mins – to include 10 x 30 seconds at Effort 4 and 5 x 1-min hill climbs at Effort 3
3. *Long run:* 6–7 miles Effort 2

3
1. *Threshold run:* 25 mins Effort 3
2. *Fartlek run:* 35 mins – include 10 x 30 seconds at Effort 4
3. *Steady run:* 35 mins Effort 2
4. *Long run:* 7–8 miles Effort 2

4
1. *Cross-training:* 40 mins
2. *Hill session:* 30 mins at Effort 2 – with 10 x 1 min hills at Effort 3, jogging back to recover
3. *Long run:* 8–9 miles, Effort 1

5
1. *Threshold run:* 30 mins Effort 3
2. *Interval run:* 40 mins including 6 x 3 min at Effort 4, with 2 min recoveries at Effort 1 and 10 mins at Effort 3 to finish
3. *Long run:* 9–10 miles Effort 2

6
1. *Steady run:* 45 mins Effort 2
2. *Hill run:* 45 mins, increasing speed to Effort 4 up hills, recovering downhill and on flat
3. *Long run:* 10–11 miles Effort 2 OR 6-9 mile race

7
1. *Interval run:* 40 mins 5 x 3 mins at Effort 4, with 2 min recoveries at Effort 1, followed by 15 mins at Effort 3
2. *Threshold run:* 25 mins Effort 3
3. *Hilly run:* 40 mins, Effort 2 including 10 x 20 second hills at Effort 4.
4. *Long run:* 11–12 miles Effort 1

8

1   *Interval run:* 40 mins 6 x 3 min faster bursts at Effort 4, with 2 mins jogging between each burst, followed by 10 mins at Effort 3

2   *Long run:* 13–14 miles Effort 1

9

1   *Threshold run:* 30 mins Effort 3

2   *Steady run:* 40 mins Effort 2

3   *Speed session :* 30 mins: 5 x 3 mins at Effort 4 with 3-min jog recovery

4   *Long run:* 14–15 miles Effort 2

10

1   *Steady run:* 1 hr 10 mins Effort 2

2   *Hill run:* 30 mins, to include 10 x 1 min uphill at Effort 4, jogging in between

3   *Long run:* 16–17 miles Effort 2 OR marathon race

11

1   *Speed session:* 30 mins: 10 x 60 seconds at Effort 4 with 60 second jog recovery, followed by 10 mins at Effort 3

2   *Threshold run:* 35 mins Effort 3

3   *Easy run:* 45 mins, Effort 1

4   *Long run:* 18–19 miles Effort 2

12

1   *Steady run:* 1hr 10 Effort 2

2   *Split Threshold Run:* 8 mins at Effort 3, 2 mins jog x 4

13

1   *Steady run:* 45 mins Effort 2

2   *Fartlek run:* 45 mins, to include 12 faster bursts of 40–60 seconds at Effort 5 and last 10 mins at Effort 3

3   *Threshold run:* 25 mins Effort 3

4   *Long run:* 19–20 miles Effort 2

14

1   *Steady run:* 40 mins Effort 2

2   *Interval run:* 20 mins to include 5 x 2 mins Effort 4 with 2 mins recovery at Effort 1

3   *Long run:* 10 miles Effort 2

15

1   *Threshold run:* 30 mins, Effort 3

2   *Easy run:* 45 mins Effort 1 including 5x 30-second hills at Effort 3

3   *Long run:* 5 miles Effort 2 with last 5 mins at Effort 3

16

1   *Easy run:* 20 mins Effort 1 with 5x 20m strides at the end

2   *Easy run:* 20 mins

3   *Race Day*

staying with it 4

∴ Keeping track

HOW TO STAY MOTIVATED AND MONITOR YOUR PROGRESS

Rule number one: accept now that there will be ups and downs in your training. Then it won't be such a shock when you experience a 'plateau', from which it seems hard to improve, or when you feel so negative about running that you can barely summon up the enthusiasm to get out the door. These fluxes in motivation, and in actual progress, are only natural, so don't be too despondent, and read on to find out how to ensure that momentary lapses or backslides don't become anything more serious....

Motivation: get it, keep it, use it!

One of the main reasons that people drop out of exercise programmes is because they don't get the results they hoped for. Sometimes, that's because the results they expected were unrealistic; other times it's because they were not training in the right manner to yield those much-wanted results. By reading and following the advice in this book, you shouldn't fall into either of these categories. But that's not to say that there won't be days when you wonder why you started this whole marathon business in the first place! If that happens, here are some strategies to help you get through....

Keep perspective

It's unlikely that anyone will get through 16 weeks without a busy period at work, a stinking cold, a niggling ache, a rip roaring hangover or simply a lapse in motivation. So don't panic, or think that a couple of days off is going to ruin everything. Equally, if you do get a bit behind on your training, don't be tempted to overcompensate by doubling up when you get back on track.

Congratulate yourself

You are already among a minority in being committed enough to start training for a marathon – acknowledge that fact and be proud of it.

Don't dwell

If you are having an 'off' period – at least try to enjoy it rather than skulking around feeling guilty. If you don't want to run on Sunday morning, then do something really enjoyable instead – don't lie in bed telling yourself what a loser you are.

Enter a race

There's nothing like a deadline to focus the mind – if your marathon deadline is still too far off to feel real, try entering another, shorter-distance race that is sooner. But remember, your finish time is not the be-all and end-all. Don't push yourself too hard, or you'll take too long to fully recover, which will have a negative effect on your true goal – attaining marathon fitness.

Add variety

Boredom is motivation's worst enemy. Avoid it by varying your training as much as you can. Don't run the same old routes every time. Go to a running camp, or visit an athletics track instead of training on the roads. If you normally run alone, go with a group – if you normally run first thing, go at dusk.

Treat yourself

The odd reward or incentive can help you feel positive about training. Treat yourself to a chiropody appointment, a massage (not a sports one, but a really indulgent one with aromatherapy oils and dolphin music!) or some new kit.

Be organised

You are much more likely to stick to your plan of running if your kit is nicely laid out on the chair, your water bottle not full of stale sports drink and your watch or HRM handily placed. Keep all your running gear in one place so you can find it easily – including socks and underwear.

Inspire yourself

Have a motivational picture on the wall/by your desk. I have a picture of Roger Bannister breaking the tape on the 4-minute mile – but you may prefer a picture of a runner in a vast scenic landscape, or of Chris Moon pushing the boundaries of human endeavour in the Marathon des Sables. You may also find that motivational music and mantras help inspire you. See page 91 for more details.

Shift focus

Rather than logging the miles, try focusing on some other measure of your progress, such as the new firmness in your thighs, your ability to stretch further, your lower resting heart rate, better sleep patterns or clearer skin. All gratifying reasons to keep on running....

Ask yourself why you are here

Why did you decide to run the marathon? Hopefully, what motivated you to enter is still important to you (whether it's to support a charity, to prove to yourself that you can, or to regain the fitness you once had). Think about what got you started and remind yourself why it's important to see this thing through.

Create a support system

Whether it is your partner, another runner, a friend, someone from the charity you are running for or even your physio, make sure you have someone – at least one person – you can talk to about your progress, your doubts and your achievements. No man or woman is an island!

Monitor your progress

Nothing is more inspiring than progress. You start off huffing and puffing around a four-mile course – now you can do six without a second thought. One of the best ways of monitoring your progress is to keep a training diary or log in which you note down the details of all your training sessions.

Your training diary can record as much or as little information as you want it to. It could simply say how long or how far you ran, and at what pace, or you could include how you felt on the run, what route you took, what the weather was like, what stretches you did afterwards and what kind of mood you were in. Research shows that people who keep a training diary are more consistent about exercise than those who don't. Designated logbooks are available from specialist sports shops or you can use a web-based log (available on many running websites); opt for a standard diary, or a simple notebook. It may take a little perseverance at first to remember to fill it in and to find a few minutes in which to do so, but eventually it will become as much a part of your routine as running itself.

Another way of monitoring progress is to repeat the tests that you performed at the start of the

programme, to see whether you now fare better. Revisit the tests on page 5 and compare your results. Write it all down in your training log!

Play mind games

As you will learn on page 91, your mind is as much involved in running as your heart, lungs and legs. The tips and strategies below are simple ways of persuading yourself to run when you aren't feeling fired up.

➢ Get up and put on your running kit. I have found this works a treat – I'll wake up and decide not to go for a run after all, but put on my kit, have a cup of tea and, before I know it, I'm thinking, 'hmm, perhaps I will just have a run….'

➢ Pledge to go out just for 10 minutes. If you genuinely feel tired or under the weather, you'll want to come back when the 10 minutes are up, but the chances are, once you've done 10 minutes you'll carry on.

➢ Don't feel like a run at all? OK, go for a walk then, but wear your running kit, just in case, and you may just find yourself breaking out into a jog.

➢ Forget your watch. The programme says 30 minutes at Level 3. Your brain says feet up in front of the TV. So, leave your watch at home, go for a run and come home when you've had enough.

➢ Listen to music. Research shows that upbeat, rhythmic music can psyche you up for physical activity. Try warming up with music on.

Train, don't strain

All these tricks and tactics to get yourself into your trainers and out the door are all very well, but if you are feeling depressed, fatigued, irritable, and if your performance seems to be taking a nosedive, you may be teetering on the brink of burnout, or 'overtraining', as the experts call it. OK, so you may not be putting in 250 km a week, like an elite distance runner, but still, in relative terms you have been pushing hard, physically and mentally and you may need to take a step back to recuperate. In fact, you absolutely should, otherwise you risk dropping out of training altogether due to burnout, illness or injury.

Signs of overtraining

- Poor performance
- Depression or irritableness
- Consistently raised resting pulse rate
- Lack of motivation
- Recurring colds, sore throats, mouth ulcers or other signs of a weakened immune system
- Problems sleeping
- Fluctuation in appetite
- General fatigue
- Irregular or absent periods (see your doctor if this persists for three months or more – this could be a sympton of amenorrhoea, which puts you at risk of weakened bones and should not be ignored).

What to do if you've overtrained

Rest. Take a whole week off – with absolutely no running – and ensure you get lots of sleep and rest. Eat healthily and don't overdo things. If you feel anxious about missing valuable training time, use the week to practise your mental tactics, start to plan your race strategy and the logistics of getting to the

event – that will ensure you feel eager to get back on track and don't lose focus. When you venture out again, try running with no stopwatch to see how you feel. If you feel back to your old self then resume training at the level at which you stepped out. Don't try to 'catch up' by doing tougher or longer sessions.

:: Two's company

RUNNING AND TRAINING WITH LIKEMINDED FOLK

One of the best things about running is that it is a totally independent pursuit. You don't need anyone to make it happen except yourself. Having said that, there are times when it is safer, more effective or more enjoyable to run with others – either a training partner, or with a group or club. But it isn't just motivation and companionship that you'll gain from joining a running group or club. You'll also get valuable advice and guidance, a whole load of new running routes and a ready source of information on such things as good local races, physios and sports shops in your area.

Finding a partner

The ideal training partner is someone of pretty much the same level as you – or, so as you don't rest on your laurels, a little better. There is absolutely no point in running with your 2 hr. 30 min. marathoning buddy if you are a novice, no matter what he or she says to the contrary. And don't partner up with someone who sees every training run as a competition between the two of you – it will be pretty well impossible to stick to a steady pace, or focus on quality, when you are secretly racing. And if it's your 'other half', it could quite likely lead to divorce proceedings!

Find the right person, though, and a training partner is a real asset. For a start, the sum total of motivation is twice as big, meaning that the chances of you ducking out of a training session are twice as small. It's also much easier to get through tough stuff, like intervals and hills, when you've got someone to commiserate with – or to shout encouraging words! And on the long runs, the time passes much more quickly when you have got somebody to talk to. On a practical level, it's also helpful to have another pair of eyes for when you are counting reps, timing an effort or following a new route. Safety is another factor to consider, particularly for female runners.

All in all, a trusty training partner – even if it's someone you run with just once or twice a week – is something every budding marathoner should aim to find. And what better place to look than your local running club?

Join the club

Before you join any running club, go along to a training session to get a feel of it – most clubs will readily allow you to do this, with no strings attached. Assess how friendly it is (is it cliquey?), whether it is a highly competitive club that expects members to race regularly, and whether there is any kind of

expertise available in the way of coaching and training programmes. Some clubs are very male-dominated, or geared mainly towards a particular age group, or type of running (such as sprinting). Find out as much as you can by talking to existing members. Most clubs will have specific training sessions, say, a track night and a long run, but some aren't so structured, so try to find one that suits your needs.

Check out the nationwide running map at *www.british-athletics.co.uk* to find your local amateur athletics club, or get the excellent annual guide *The Rundown* (see 'Further Information').

Sisters are doing it for themselves

Some women, especially when starting out, prefer to train in the company of other women. That's why the *Women's Running Network*, was set up in 1999 – it now has more than 30 groups across the UK to help women of all ages and abilities get into running and continue making progress. Some groups operate dedicated marathon training programmes. See 'Further Information' for more details.

Virtual clubs and forums

If you don't want – or can't find – a training partner, but you'd still like to monitor your progress, swap notes and get advice from other runners, consider joining a virtual running group, such as *www.runningmates.co.uk*, or registering onto a forum, such as the one on the Runner's World or Real Runner's websites. That way, you'll get some support and feedback, but you won't have to make conversation if you don't feel like it!

Running away

Until you become a runner yourself, you are unaware of the vast network of fellow runners that exists

around the world. I was amazed when I first learned of 'marathon training camps' a few years ago, but now I know that everything from weekend 'technique' clinics to point-to-point runs in exotic locations, yoga and running weekends and warm-weather training camps are all there for the taking. It's a great way of meeting other runners, as well as getting some useful training advice and practice, and it's the kind of holiday that you can easily go on alone without looking like a sad single! (See 'Further Information' for more details).

Canine companions

The training partner I most often run with is of the four-legged variety – my dog Sidney. Running with him is the perfect compromise between being totally alone and feeling obliged to socialise. It also saves me having to take him out walking, as well as finding time to fit in a run. Special dog leads, which attach around the waist, are available for running with your dog so that you can keep your arms free, but you can always improvise by cutting a long portion of lead from one of those extendable leads and securing it loosely around your waist.

why we are here

Walking is a great form of exercise for health, but running is better: a study in the *Journal of the American Medical Association* found that the risk of type 2 diabetes was substantially lower in women who did more vigorous activities than in those who walked.

Doggie dos and don'ts

- Don't run with a dog younger than six months – his bones and muscles aren't fully developed yet.

- Don't run with a dog that is old or overweight.

- Only take your dog running if he is obedient enough to respond to commands.

- Remember that dogs need hydrating too. Many of our routes take in rivers or streams, so Sid can stop for a drink, but if you aren't going to pass anywhere appropriate it's important to carry water for your canine pal. Also ensure there is a fresh bowl of water for your dog on your return.

- Don't take a dog running in very hot weather, since they can't regulate body temperature as well as we can. Warning signs of over-exertion include excessive panting, slowing down and a dry tongue.

- Don't force the dog. Start your dog off with shorter runs and stick to softer surfaces.

- Not all breeds are suited to running; other dogs just don't enjoy it. Breeds such as border collies, Springer spaniels, larger terriers and hunting dogs are ideally built; Bassett hounds are not!

- Speak to your vet if you are in doubt about your dog's suitability for running.

why we are here

Regular running increases the number and size of mitochondria in our muscles by up to 35 per cent – these 'engine rooms' are where energy metabolism takes place. The more mitochondria, the greater the body's ability to extract and utilise oxygen.

∴ Training without the trainers

MAKING USE OF YOUR GREY MATTER TO BE A BETTER RUNNER

When elite athletes line up on the start line of a race, there's very little to choose between them in terms of their physical fitness and readiness to perform. Who wins and loses is largely down to the athletes' psychological skills and mental toughness. That's why they spend hours mentally 'rehearsing' their sport, mastering mental tricks and strategies to reduce anxiety or psyche themselves up to perform, and learning how to remain focused, motivated and positive. But can common-or-garden budding marathoners benefit from this, too? You bet they can.

This section will guide you through some of the most useful psychological strategies, both for preparing for your marathon and performing on the day. But a word of warning: these techniques take practice – it's no use attempting them for the first time on race day morning, the more you practise, the more benefit you'll gain – even in the case of the techniques that are geared towards race day itself.

Tuning in versus switching off

When you run, do you think about what you're going to have for dinner, look at the window displays in the high street shops, chat to fellow runners and generally focus on anything other than your running? If so, you are what sport psychologist William Morgan called a 'disassociator', who focuses externally. If, in contrast, you naturally tune into the rhythm of your footfall, the feel of your muscles contracting, and the sound of your breathing, you are an 'associator' – someone who 'internalises' their focus and remains in tune with their body's feedback signals.

Research suggests that accomplished marathon runners are more likely to be associators, while less proficient runners are more often disassociators during racing – but that in training, it's a different story. In one study, 43 per cent of elite runners used just disassociative strategies when training, 21 per cent used just associative and 36 per cent used both. It's as if during the long hard days of training the athletes feel the need to tune out of the physical experience somewhat, while when it really counts, on race day, they need to remain focused internally.

So, if you feel the need to disassociate during the long months of training – distract yourself by listening to music, watching TV, chatting or exercising in a pleasant location. But don't switch off too much, or your technique might suffer, and you may miss the early warning signs of an overuse injury. As far as racing goes, try making like a pro, and practise association.

Seeing is believing

Without doubt one of the most regularly used cognitive (mental) strategies is visualisation, or mental imagery. It is now widely established that the use of mental imagery can actually enhance physical performance. It's all to do with 'seeing is believing'. In effect, the brain cannot tell the difference between something that has actually happened and a vivid mental picture of it happening. In marathon terms, if you can't picture yourself crossing that finish line, you're far less likely to put everything into achieving it, and therefore less likely to succeed. Conversely, picture yourself doing it proficiently and it's almost as if it is a fait accompli.

Now imagine that you've just passed the 26-mile marker – you've got 285 yards to go. What will it look like, as you hit that home straight? Picture the crowds – maybe you'll have your own family or friends there to watch you finish. Imagine the sounds of people cheering, announcements being made over the loudspeaker.... Use all your senses to create a vivid image – visual, auditory, kinaesthetic (feel), taste and smell. Also try to imagine your state of mind, or mood. Think about how you would like to feel, both in terms of your body and your mind – you'll be tired, yes, but elated and delighted with your success. Put it all together into a vivid image and see yourself crossing that finish line. What does the time say on the clock? Be precise. Visualise the figures on the clock, the hours, minutes and seconds.

Once you've achieved this – repeat it regularly. Scientists at the University of Lyon demonstrated that the more proficient the imagery skill, the greater the benefit to performance.

Make it work

Practise somewhere quiet, comfortable, and when you are in a relaxed state. You may prefer to close your eyes. When you have finished, take a few breaths, then open your eyes and take a moment to re-adjust. Limit your visualisations to 1 to 3 minutes and repeat often for maximum effect.

Mind games on the run

Sometimes we could all use a little extra help when we're out running, to get through the tough moments. These simple psychological techniques can be practised on the move...

Change your orientation

Instead of worrying about the outcome of the race or training run, focus on the process and the individual steps that need to be taken to get to the end. For example, think about getting to the next street corner (or mile marker in a race), or up the next hill. That way you retain focus on the 'here and now' and quit worrying about the final result.

Use a mantra

Some people find it helpful to have a mantra related to their sports performance. A mantra is simply a key word or phrase on which to focus, to prevent negative thoughts slipping in and to drip-feed your subconscious mind with positive affirmations about your abilities. It might be, 'I am a strong and capable runner' or 'I can cross the finish line with a smile on my face'. Mantras aren't just for posting up on the fridge and saying in the bath – they can be used while you're actually out training and racing, too. 'I am running fast and strong,' is one I use when I'm actually out running – it has a nice rhythm to it.

Switch strategies

If you're associating, and the focus on your body is getting too uncomfortable, try disassociating. If you're feeling unmotivated and 'not present' in your running, you are probably too disassociated, so try associating by focusing on your breathing, your arms pumping, the ground moving steadily under your feet. It sometimes helps to count in time with your breath to get into an associated frame of mind.

fuelling up 5

⸫ Getting the basics right

THE GENERAL PRINCIPLES OF GOOD NUTRITION AND HOW TO PUT THEM INTO PRACTICE

Imagine a top motor racing driver on the front row of the grid before the start of a race: he may be the best driver in the world, in the best car, but if his car contains poor quality fuel, or if he has failed to top up the tank, his performance will invariably suffer. The same is true of the human body – no matter how well trained you are, and how well you have prepared, if your body contains poor quality fuel, or not enough of it, your running won't be up to scratch.

The fuel that your body needs for normal function, daily activity and exercise comes from the food and drink that you consume. While the amount of energy you need is an important factor, and one we will look at shortly, the quality of your energy intake is crucial to optimal performance.

Most runners know that carbohydrate is the key fuel for runners. However, that doesn't mean that fat and protein aren't also essential nutrients. Nor does it mean that all carbohydrate sources are as good as each other. Let's take a closer look at the main nutrients in turn, so as to determine their role in good health and great running.

Fat – is it really the bad guy?

Most of us have plenty of fat stored on our bodies – enough, in fact, to run more than 20 consecutive marathons! Not only do we eat a higher than necessary amount of fat in our diet (the average British diet contains 40 per cent fat), but many of us consume too many calories overall, and so the surplus energy is converted to fat and stored. While training can help you utilise fat as a fuel more efficiently, that isn't a reason for scoffing down lots of it. For starters, being overweight increases the risk of heart disease and diabetes. It has also been associated with some types of cancer, including breast cancer. Fat also requires less energy to be metabolised than either carbohydrate or protein, so is more likely to end up as body fat. Besides, when you are running 26.2 miles, you certainly won't want to be carrying any extra weight than you have to!

That said, fat is an essential nutrient and it does have an important role to play in a balanced diet. Certain vitamins, A, D, E and K, are fat-soluble, so can be derived only from fat sources. In addition, fat provides insulation and protection for our bodies and, for women, it enables pregnancy and lactation to take place.

How much, what type?

Fat contains 9 kilocalories per gram, compared to carbohydrate and protein which both contain approximately 4 kilocalories per gram. Immediately you can see that fat is a very energy-dense food, and is easy to over-consume. The UK government recommends that we aim to reduce fat intake to 33-35 per cent of our overall calorie intake, but you may want to consider going a little lower in the name of marathon training – I would recommend striving for perhaps 25 per cent of your overall intake. So, for example, if you consume 3,000 calories per day in training, that means 750 calories can come from fat sources. And, since we know that 1 g of fat = 9 calories, that means 83 g of fat per day.

Fat comes in three main forms in our diet. All are constructed from three fatty acids attached to a unit of glycerol – and collectively this unit is called a triglyceride. While all of them, gram for gram, have the same number of calories, they differ greatly in their roles in human health.

Saturated fatty acids

As far as your health is concerned, saturated fats are bad news, encouraging the body to produce more of the low-density lipoproteins (LDL cholesterol) and also being associated with a greater risk of some cancers. Experts recommend that no more than 10 per cent of total calorie intake should be consumed as saturated fats. So, for example, if you eat 2,500 calories per day, only 250 should come from saturated fat sources, which include meat, butter, dairy products, pastry, coconut and palm oil (often in peanut butter and processed snacks such as flapjacks).

Polyunsaturated fats

In general, polyunsaturated fats take a middle road in terms of health, since they lower LDL cholesterol and the risk of heart disease, but also lower the good guy cholesterol, high density lipoproteins (HDL). However, there are two essential fatty acids that come under the polyunsaturated umbrella: they are called 'essential' because they cannot be made by the body but are vital to health.

Omega 6 fatty acids, or linoleic acids, come from vegetable oil, polyunsaturated margarine and products made from it. Omega 6s reduce LDL but, if consumed excessively, also may reduce HDL levels, as well as increasing the damage done by 'free radicals' linked to cancer.

Omega 3 fatty acids, or linolenic acids, have no such negative effects and are in fact positively beneficial to health, reducing the risk of blood clotting, stroke, heart disease and controlling inflammation. They therefore can be helpful in dealing with diseases such as arthritis. The major source is oily fish but you can also get significant amounts from some nuts, including walnuts, linseed and its oils and dark green leafy vegetables such as kale and spinach. On the whole, we consume a lot more omega 6 than omega 3, and it is recommended that the balance is shifted the other way for better health.

Monounsaturated fats

These are distinguishable because they are liquid at room temperature, but solid when chilled (that's why French dressing if made with olive oil goes solid in the fridge). Studies show that replacing saturated fats with monounsaturates in the diet reduces the risk of heart disease. The beauty is that they lower LDL levels while maintaining HDL levels. They also appear to limit free radical damage. Aim for 12 per cent of total energy intake. The best sources are olive oil, rapeseed oil, nut oils, avocados, nuts and seeds.

Trans fats

Trans fats do not occur in significant amounts in nature, but are created by adding extra hydrogen to polyunsaturated fatty acids. The chemical process by which this takes place makes them at least as bad for health as saturated fats, increasing LDL and lowering HDL cholesterol. These fats are found mainly in processed foods, such as fried fast food, biscuits and cakes, and in hard margarine. Keep intake to a minimum.

Another reason to up your omega 3s!

A study on fat intake found that omega 3 fatty acids could enhance aerobic metabolism, improving the delivery of oxygen and nutrients to cells by reducing the viscosity of the blood and the condition of the red blood cells that carry haemoglobin to the cells. It may also help you recover from the rigours of training, by reducing the inflammation in muscles, tendons and ligaments associated with hard exercise.

Get your fats right

So what does it all mean to you? Well, in general it means cutting down on fat generally, and specifically cutting down saturated and trans fats, so that a greater proportion of your dietary fat comes from monounsaturated and polyunsaturated sources (particularly the omega 3s). Outlawing certain foods – whatever their fat content – isn't the way to go. If you love a biscuit with your cup of tea, or if fish and chips are your favourite indulgence, then simply eat them less frequently and make healthier choices elsewhere in your diet.

Cutting out dairy products in order to trim calories isn't a wise move, either, since these are the richest source of calcium, which has an essential role in muscle contraction and in metabolism. It's also vital in maintaining bone health, since calcium is a component of bone.

Protein

You don't have to be a bodybuilder or a sports scientist to know that protein is associated with muscles and strength. Dissect a muscle, and you'll find it consists almost entirely of protein. As far as your training is concerned, protein does not have a major role in energy production but it is part of the structure of every cell in the body. Sufficient dietary protein is essential for maintaining normal body maintenance, transporting oxygen around the body, regulating fluid balance, repairing tissues, playing a role in metabolism and muscular contraction, and is a component of many of the body's enzymes, hormones and neurotransmitters. Proteins are constructed from substances called amino acids, of which there are 20, all with distinctive functions within the body. Of these 20, eight are termed 'essential' amino acids, because they must be supplied by the diet and cannot be made from other amino acids.

How much, what type?

With protein playing such a significant role in muscle tissue maintenance and repair, it follows that someone in heavy training needs more than the average Joe does. For a start, the increased breakdown of protein during training needs to be compensated for, and in addition, if glycogen stores are low (say, towards the end of your long run) certain amino acids – called branch chain amino acids – can be used for energy. While using protein as a fuel source isn't an ideal scenario, it is an essential fall-back when glycogen stores are depleted. Research shows that the increased need for protein among active people is particularly significant at the outset of training, since the body has yet to become accustomed to conserving and recycling protein.

So how much is enough? Guidelines for the general public recommend that protein intake should equal 0.75 g per kg of body weight. However, if you've just embarked on your marathon training programme, you should aim to increase your intake to 1.2 to 1.4 g per kg of body weight. This in general should equate to around 15 per cent of your total energy intake.

Carbohydrate

Whether you are a budding marathoner or your idea of sport is darts and snooker, the majority of your energy should come from carbohydrates. So why are carbs so important? The main reason is that they provide the body's supply of glycogen, which is stored in the liver and muscles and is the fuel that powers your running. Since only a limited amount can be stored – and since carbohydrate is the only fuel your brain can use – supplies need to be constantly replenished. Too little dietary carbohydrate, and you will not be firing on all cyclinders. Carbs also pack a micronutrient-fuelled punch – being rich in B vitamins, iron, magnesium and chromium.

How much, what type?

A typical sedentary person consumes 40 to 50 per cent of total calories in the form of carbohydrate – active people should aim to increase this to closer to 60 per cent of daily calories. But what type? There was a time when carbohydrate was defined in terms of 'starches' and 'sugars'. The premise was that starches were good, and sugars bad. Starches included such foods as bread, pasta and potatoes, and some other vegetables, while sugars included sugary snacks and drinks, sweets, table sugar, fruits and some vegetables. But more recent research has revealed that the 'good and bad' argument isn't that simple. The real issue is the rate of absorption of a carbohydrate-rich food, and its consequent effect on the speed at which blood sugar levels rise, measured by the 'glycaemic index (GI)'. The faster that blood sugar rises, the more insulin that needs to be released to carry it out of the blood; and, since insulin acts as the 'gatekeeper' to the fat cells, the greater the chance of it being stored as fat. If you opt for foods that give a less steep blood sugar curve this will enable energy levels to be maintained and also allow the body to burn fat as a fuel more efficiently.

But bear in mind that GI is a measurement of how fast and how high blood sugar and insulin rise after you eat enough of a food to total 50 g of carbohydrate. For example, white bread and carrots have high GI numbers of 70 and 71 respectively, suggesting that they both send blood sugar soaring. But, since a slice of white bread contains 18.9 g of carbohydrate and a standard portion of carrots (80 g, or a handful) contains 3.1 g of carbohydrate, you would have to eat 16 handfuls of carrots to get 50 g of carbohydrate, whereas you would only need to eat 2.5 slices of bread to get the same amount.

The other point that is often overlooked is that we rarely eat foods on their own, and that there are many factors that mitigate the effect on blood sugar levels, such as the presence of fibre and protein, and of acids.

So how can you determine a food's GI? Well, I'm afraid it's a matter of looking up foods in reference books. While many of the runner's staples – bagels, baked potatoes, pasta, rice and breakfast cereal – have a high glycaemic index, recent research suggests that highly active, fit people have a less pronounced response to high glycaemic index foods and so don't have to worry so much about their

effects on blood sugar. However, opting for mainly wholegrains, wholemeal bread, pasta and rice, pulses and beans, and eating a wide range of fruits and vegetables, should ensure a sustained energy supply as well as a nutritionally rich diet.

Don't run on empty

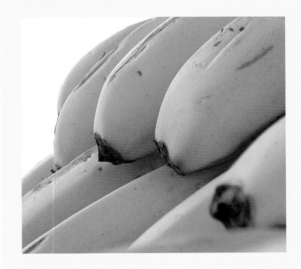

If you haven't eaten since lunchtime and are running straight after work or early evening, you'll need something to tide you over and provide the fuel necessary for your workout. Why? To prevent low blood sugar (hypoglycaemia), which could leave you feeling tired, dizzy and light headed, and certainly won't contribute to good performance. A snack an hour before your run will provide readily accessible fuel for your muscles, take the edge off hunger and make you feel alert and psyched up for a run. A banana, a handful of raisins, a couple of Ryvitas with peanut butter, or half a bagel will all do the trick. A recent study, published in the *Exercise Immunology Review*, also found that taking carbohydrate on board before exercise helps to mitigate the decreased immune function associated with heavy training.

:• A question of calories

WORKING OUT HOW MUCH ENERGY YOU NEED TO MAINTAIN, LOSE OR GAIN WEIGHT

Now that we've looked at the basics of good nutrition, you might be wondering whether you are eating enough – or too much – to optimise your performance. There's a very simple equation when it comes to maintaining your body weight: calories in = calories out = steady weight.

If 'calories out' exceed 'calories in', you'll lose weight; and if 'calories in' exceed 'calories out', you'll gain weight. Simple, huh? But how do you know how many calories you need, and indeed, how many you are expending through your training and other activities? Thankfully, it's not too difficult to find out. Read on to find out more....

Make a quick recovery

After a long run, make sure you eat some carbohydrate within half an hour of finishing, so as to refill your glycogen stores. Studies have shown that this is the perfect 'window' to allow maximum absorption of the carbohydrate – if you wait until you've showered and stretched that window will have closed. Foods that are moderate to high on the glycaemic index will work fastest. Aim to eat 1 g of carbohydrate for every kg of your body weight to optimise refuelling, and take some protein on board with your carbs for maximum benefit.

How much do you need?

How much energy you need is determined by three things: your resting metabolic rate (RMR), which is the minimum number of calories needed to survive, even if you stayed in bed all day long; the 'thermic effect of food', which is the energy needed to digest what you eat; and, finally, energy for daily activity, whether that be washing the dishes or doing your long run. To get a rough idea of how many calories you need, grab a calculator and do the following sums:

1 *My weight in kilograms (1 kilogram = 2.2 lb)*

2 *Females*
I am 18–30 years old: weight x 14.7. Answer + 496 = RMR OR
I am 31–60 years old: weight x 8.7. Answer + 829 = RMR

Males
I am18–30 years old: weight x 15.3. Answer + 679 = RMR OR
I am 31–60 years old: weight x 11.6. Answer + 879 = RMR

My estimated RMR is

3 *Take this figure and multiply it by the number below most closely representing your typical daily activity level.*
I am sedentary (sit or stand most of the day)   *1.4*
I am moderately active (some walking each day
and regular active leisure time activities)   *1.7*
I am very active (physically active each day)   *2.0*

My result is

Now let's think about the calories you expend running. A very broad guideline to the number of calories expended through running is 100 calories per mile. Remember, though, that running uphill and off-road on soft or uneven surfaces uses more calories.

If you want a more accurate picture of the energy you burn through running, use the following calculation:

Body weight in kg x average weekly distance in km's x 1.036 [Ans]/7 (in order to get a daily amount).

In terms of marathon training, if you are running, say, 30 miles a week, you will expend around 3,000 calories more than if you were sedentary. That breaks down to 430 calories per day extra needed, assuming that you are a stable weight and happy with that weight. Ensure that the extra energy you take on board is good quality food and drink and not chocolate bars and biscuits. Remember, too, that if you use sports drinks you may already be supplying a significant amount of these extra calories.

But I want to lose weight!

If you embark on a serious marathon training programme and do not increase your calorie intake you will almost certainly lose weight, but there's a fine line between shedding unwanted pounds and failing to provide your body all the energy it needs to fuel training and recovery. Do not attempt to follow a strict calorie-controlled diet and marathon train simultaneously. You'll end up feeling exhausted and depressed, your running will suffer and you put yourself at risk of illness and ill-health through a lack of vitamins and minerals, as well as possibly dehydration.

These tips will assist your weight loss efforts:

- Cut down on high-fat and processed or highly refined foods, particularly saturated fats, manufactured snacks, cakes, crisps and biscuits, hard cheese, fatty cuts of meat and alcohol.

- Add resistance training to your running regime to increase muscle mass and, therefore, metabolic rate.

- Ensure you stay hydrated – otherwise you may mistake thirst signals for hunger.

- Make liquid foods a regular aspect of your diet – research from Penn State University showed that these are more filling than drier foods of the same calorie content. For example, thick carrot soup instead of raw carrots, a fruit smoothie rather than a banana.

- Only use energy drinks, gels or bars on or after long runs – not as routine.

- Keep healthy snacks at the ready – if you come in from a run feeling ravenous, you'll want something to munch on quickly, so ensure you have a range of healthy choices.

why we are here

Running gives us the opportunity to face the elements, breathe fresh air and see greenery, fulfilling an innate need to immerse ourselves in nature that ecopsychologists call 'biophilia'. Studies show that this boosts serotonin levels, making us feel more calm and content, and that it promotes healing.

⁘ Fluid thinking

THE IMPORTANCE OF FLUID BEFORE, DURING AND AFTER RUNNING.

The human body comprises 60 per cent water, which bathes and nourishes every cell, transports nutrients, cushions and protects organs and joints, and generally keeps us alive and kicking. Even if you barely lifted a finger, your body would need 2 to 2.5 litres per day of fluid for normal function, so it quickly becomes evident that, as a marathoner in training, your needs are even greater.

Maintaining fluid balance

Strenuous exercise – like running – generates 20 times more heat than when you are at rest. We have to dissipate that heat somehow, to regulate and stabilise body temperature. The body's favoured method of losing heat is through sweating, which, of course, causes water loss through the skin. The average marathoner sweats more than 1 litre per hour during running – and if this fluid isn't replenished, dehydration will set in, causing a raised heart rate, increased blood pressure, a far higher rate of perception of effort and, ultimately, a decline in performance. To offset fluid loss resulting from exercise, you need to think about drinking before, during and after training sessions and races.

In an ideal world, a runner would consume the same volume of fluid that they lost through sweating, but studies show that replacing 80 per cent of what we've lost is a more achievable target. You can get a good idea of this volume through weighing yourself before and after a training session to see how much weight has been lost (yes, it's all fluid – not fat!). More often than not though, this isn't practical, so you need to follow some general guidelines about how much to consume.

Before you run

If you start your training session or race underhydrated, you'll be fighting a losing battle trying to compensate later. And guys be warned: research by world fitness organisation IDEA shows that men are more likely to be dehydrated at the start of a workout than women. Your hydration strategy should begin long before you start lacing up your trainers (a couple of days before, in the case of the marathon itself). Aim to drink 250 to 500 ml of water or sports drink 15 to 30 minutes before your session begins, depending on your tolerance of fluids, and the temperature and humidity.

During your run

While you are running, aim to drink 100 to 200 ml every 15 minutes. If you don't want to contend with measurements and figures, aim for 8 mouthfuls every 15 minutes. But use your common sense: if you feel thirsty, drink. If your stomach is already sloshing around with water, don't. A report in the *British*

Medical Journal warned that over-consumption of fluid (either water or sports drinks) before, during, or after exercise is unnecessary and can have a potentially fatal outcome. Further, a study by researchers at the University of Cape Town found that cyclists who were forced to replace their total sweat loss in fluid intake actually performed worse than when they drank instinctively.

After your run

Rehydration is one of the important components of recovery. As soon as you have finished your run, drink water, sports drink, or fruit juice – or eat a water-packed fruit, such as melon or grapes. Regardless of how long or intense your session was, you should drink at least half a litre of fluid after your run. If you exercised for an hour or more, aim for a litre (but sip it, rather than attempt to down it in one), and keep drinking regularly for the next few hours.

Drink up!

You may feel as if you can run quite comfortably without taking any fluid on board. But, as your training gets more challenging, you will not be optimising your performance if you fail to drink on the run. A level of just 2 per cent dehydration will noticeably affect your running, while a 4 per cent drop in hydration results in a massive 25 per cent drop in performance.

What's your tipple?

The 2 litres or '8 glasses a day' mantra is one that most of us are familiar with when it comes to water intake. But a number of respected experts have recently challenged the notion that the 2 to 2.5 litres of fluid our bodies need each day must come from water alone. As Professor Heinz Valtin, a kidney specialist, points out, at least a third of our daily fluid requirements are met by solid food, while juice, milk, soft drinks and, yes, even tea and coffee also contribute. We've been warned for so long about the pitfalls of the diuretic effect of caffeinated drinks that many of us avoid them. But it seems that the diuretic effect of caffeine has been very much overplayed. Professor Maughan, one of the UK's top hydration researchers, says, 'Caffeine is a diuretic, but the fluid provided in the drink is enough to offset its diuretic effect. Take 60 mg of caffeine and add it to a cupful of water and milk, and you'll likely end up more hydrated than if you hadn't drunk it.' In fact there may be some positive benefits to taking caffeine on board before a training run or race, which you can read about on page 108. Since it's unlikely that you'll be sipping café latte during your training runs, let's look at what type of fluid you need to take on board while you are actually on the move.

The primary function of drinking on the run is to stave off hydration. Contribution to energy supply is also a factor, and while research shows fairly conclusively that isotonic sports drinks will keep you going longer than plain water, this consideration is relevant only on longer runs (an hour or more), or when you are training very heavily and need to refuel between sessions. Sports drinks or 'isotonic' drinks contain 4 to 8 per cent (or 4 to 8 g per 100 ml) carbohydrate and are designed for rapid absorption. As well as containing some carbohydrate, isotonic drinks also have a very small amount of sodium and potassium (known as electrolytes).

This precise combination of carbohydrate and electrolytes has been shown to maximise the rate at which the drink is absorbed by the body, offsetting dehydration and providing easily accessible energy, so is ideal for drinking while on the run. A study of recreational runners, published in the *Journal of Applied Physiology*, found a 27 per cent increase in time to exhaustion with an isotonic drink compared to a 'sham' drink. A study that looked at 98 marathon runners compared the effects of a sports drink and a placebo, drunk at the rate of one litre an hour during a marathon: the runners who got the real thing were able to work at a higher heart rate, especially during the last 10 km of the race (when most people begin to slow down).

How do I know when I'm hydrated?

The simplest way of ensuring that you are properly hydrated is to check the colour of your urine. It should be a pale, straw colour – but some things will affect the colour, such as vitamin B supplements. Professor Valtin recommends following your customary fluid intake and heeding your thirst; if you are healthy and producing urine of a moderately yellow colour you should be fine, he says. The volume of urine is also important – if you are producing only small amounts and have to visit the loo only every few hours, you are probably dehydrated, regardless of the colour. See the box opposite for other telltale signs of dehydration.

Too much of a good thing

There's been a lot of media coverage regarding the issue of drinking water during endurance events, following a number of cases of 'hyponatremia', a potentially fatal condition in which the sodium concentration in the blood drops excessively due to too much water in the bloodstream. Fifteen runners in the 2003 Flora London marathon were diagnosed with hyponatremia. Research thus far suggests that women are more vulnerable to hyponatremia than men. As a safety precaution, if you predict that you will be running for four hours or more, try to consume isotonic drinks rather than water, to prevent a drop in sodium – you could even try consuming a salty snack, such as pretzels or Ryvita.

And on race day, don't drink the whole of each bottle or sachet of fluid you pick up; take a little, and throw away or carry the rest.

Dehydration alert!

- Fatigue.
- Headache.
- Poor performance.
- Dizziness.
- Lack of urination.
- Muscle cramps.
- Confusion.

What to look for in an isotonic sports drink

- A 6 to 8 per cent carbohydrate solution is optimal for release into the bloodstream. Any higher, and it is an 'energy' drink, which won't provide energy quickly enough to utilise during the run itself.

- Electrolytes: sodium and potassium salts lost through sweating.

- A taste and consistency that you like (for example, gel, liquid, powder). Research shows that flavour dictates how much an exerciser will drink during a session.

What about alcohol?

While you don't see many runners puffing away on cigarettes after a race, quite a few will be heading for the local pub for a drink. And that is absolutely fine, but there are a few points to bear in mind. First, alcohol is calorific. A pint of bitter weighs in at 175 calories, a 440 ml can of premium lager at 260, and a 175 ml glass of red wine (the standard pub measurement) at 115 calories. And even if the drink itself isn't a calorie issue for you, a study in the *American Journal of Clinical Nutrition* found that in 52 volunteers a single pre-lunch wine or beer resulted in an increased calorie intake over the next 24 hours.

Second, alcohol cannot be used directly by the muscles – it travels straight into the bloodstream from where it has to be metabolised before the body can make use of more preferable fuel sources, such as carbohydrate or fat. Consume it too regularly and it will suppress fat oxidation and promote fat storage – the exact opposite of what you want. Alcohol is also a diuretic, causing your body to lose water and increasing the likelihood of dehydration.

So, however guilty you feel, don't run with a hangover. It affects your capacity to exercise, causing palpitations, interfering with body temperature control, dulling reflexes and perception of effort. Furthermore, it's not wise to drink alcohol straight after a heavy training session or race for other reasons: alcohol has been shown to interfere with muscle repair and recovery, even when drunk 24 to 36 hours later.

why we are here

Running is one of the best ways of staying in shape for life. A recent study from Arizona State University found that highly active women over 35 years old had a far higher resting metabolic rate than their sedentary counterparts.

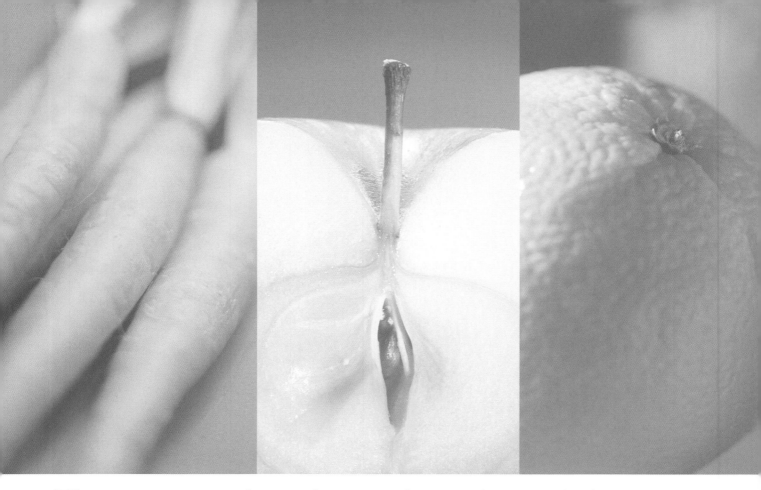

⁖ The extras: vitamins, minerals and the rest

WHO NEEDS EXTRAS? SPECIAL DIETARY CONSIDERATIONS, PLUS RUNNING ON A SPECIAL DIET.

We'd all be rattling if we took the myriad pills, potions and powders that are allegedly going to help us run faster, from vitamins and minerals to ergogenic aids and dietary supplements.... But what does the evidence say? And if your diet isn't 'normal', are there further considerations to bear in mind?

Vitamins & Minerals

Provided that you are eating a healthy balanced diet, following the principles outlined in this section, you should be getting sufficient quantities of vitamins and minerals in your diet. There is no harm, however, in taking a multi-vitamin and mineral supplement as an insurance policy – the Harvard Medical School suggests that most people would benefit from a daily multi-vitamin complex, particularly if you don't eat the recommended five portions of fruit and vegetables each day, if you are a vegan, or if you regularly miss meals or rely on highly processed foods. Keeping this in mind, let's have a look at a couple of specific vitamins and minerals that have been shown to have an influence on physical performance or recovery, and who might be at risk of deficiency.

Calcium

Calcium is best known for its role in bone building, and there is no doubt that calcium deficiency is bad news for anyone who is regularly running, and putting the skeletal system under stress. Women in particular should be vigilant about calcium intake, since a third of women post-menopause are affected by osteoporosis, a condition in which the bones become thin and fragile (see pages 156-7 for information and advice). The recommended daily allowance is 800 mg – but women who are pregnant, breast-feeding or post-menopause should increase this to 10,000 mg. The major source of calcium in the diet is dairy products – those who avoid dairy products or who are vegans should seek out calcium-enriched alternatives, such as fortified soy products, nuts and seeds, or dark green leafy vegetables. Fish with bones in (such as canned sardines or salmon) are also good sources.

Iron

Iron is an essential mineral in the human body – it is involved in the formation of red blood cells and the carrying of oxygen to all the body's cells. Insufficient iron can hamper athletic performance by allowing haemoglobin to fall below optimal levels, but you don't have to be anaemic to have low iron levels. A study in the *American Journal of Clinical Nutrition* found that iron deficiency without anaemia occurred in 12 per cent of pre-menopausal women in the United States, and had a negative effect on aerobic training. The study's authors report that iron supplementation improved performance significantly. Those most at risk of deficiency are women (due to menstruation), those on low calorie diets (who are more at risk of deficiencies of any type), vegetarians and vegans. The latter two are susceptible because 'haem' iron sources from meat and fish are better absorbed than plant-derived sources. Men should consume 8.7 mg of iron a day; women, 14.8 mg per day.

Magnesium

Magnesium is an important mineral in muscle and nerve function and has a role in bone formation. A recent US study found that magnesium-deficient women burned 15 per cent more oxygen and had higher heart rates while exercising than women with sufficient magnesium in their diets, making their workouts feel harder. Make sure you get plenty of wholegrains, nuts and seeds and green vegetables to keep magnesium levels topped up – and consider a supplement if you drink a lot of alcohol, which can hamper absorption. Men should consume 300 mg per day; women should aim for 270 mg per day.

Vitamin C

Vitamin E, like vitamins A and C, is an antioxidant, protecting against free radical damage that is actually increased as a result of exercise. A number of studies have shown that vitamin E supplementation can reduce oxidative damage caused by intense exercise. There is no current recommended intake in the UK but the EU's 'reference intake' is 10 mg a day. Rich sources include avocadoes, nuts and seeds, oily fish and vegetable oils.

Ergogenic aids

Surveys suggest that half of all runners use nutritional supplements, but the evidence supporting many of these is scant, to say the least, and such supplements may only serve to decrease your bank balance rather than increase your performance. Here are some you might fare better with.

Caffeine

Studies have shown quite conclusively that exercise performance can be enhanced in events lasting more than 90 minutes when caffeine is consumed. Tests at the Australian Institute of Sport in Canberra found that athletes who took a small quantity of caffeine could exercise up to 30 per cent longer than those who took a placebo. It was initially believed that this was due to it promoting fat utilisation, thereby sparing glycogen for later in the session. But recent research suggests that caffeine prevents the rise in neurotransmitters associated with fatigue during exercise, so you simply don't feel tired.

While coffee gets a bad press for its dehydrating and diuretic effect on sports people, studies have shown that caffeine consumption prior to exercise neither increases urination or dehydration, possibly due to high levels of adrenaline interfering with the usual effect on the kidneys.

So how much do you need to get a performance benefit? A sensible guideline is 2 mg per lb of body weight of caffeine, an hour before you run, equating to roughly 2 to 3 cups of coffee for most people. You would exceed the legal limit of 12 mcg of caffeine per 1ml of urine only if you drank, say, four large double shot cappuccinos, or 16 cans of coke before you ran. Caffeine pills, such as *ProPlus,* work too.

Conjugated linoleic acid (CLA)

CLA is an omega 6 fatty acid, currently causing a stir in research circles, since it seems to be able to increase the rate at which we burn fat, while simultaneously inhibiting fat storage. It works best when combined with regular exercise, studies suggest. One research project found that 1.8 g per day, combined with 90 minutes' exercise 3 days a week for 12 weeks, resulted in a 20 per cent decrease in body fat. No side effects have yet been found – so it may be worth a try if you are battling with your weight during your marathon training.

Glucosamine sulphate

Glucosamine sulphate is a naturally occurring substance in the body, which plays a role in keeping cartilage healthy and reducing 'wear and tear' on joints. Many sportspeople have latched on to the idea of taking additional glucosamine in the form of supplements to prevent or lessen joint pain and osteoarthritis. Recent studies have vilified this idea, showing quite significant improvements in pain levels after supplementation. For example, a study published in the *British Journal of Sports Medicine* found that 2,000 mg taken for 12 weeks provided pain relief and improved function in 88 per cent of subjects with knee pain. Other research suggests 1,000 to 1,500 mg a day is sufficient, and that the product works best when taken in conjunction with chondroitin (many supplements contain both – check the label).

Special Diets

There are a few added challenges related to eating healthily during marathon training if you follow a restricted or special diet, one that excludes certain foods or food groups. While it is beyond the realms of this book to go into great detail about specific diets, here are some areas that particular groups should be especially aware of.

Vegetarians

Vegetarians are, in general, less likely to suffer from heart disease and cancer than meat eaters, but avoiding meat and fish could lead to sub-optimal iron and zinc intake and to low levels of omega 3 fatty acids, which are abundant in oily fish. It also means that you need to think more carefully about your protein sources, since only animal-derived foods can offer the full range of essential amino acids. To get your full complement of amino acids on a vegetarian diet, you need to combine two different plant-based foods, such as serving lentils with rice, peanut butter with wholemeal bread, a soya or quorn food with pasta, or a dairy food with wholegrain cereals. Here are a few other tips to ensure you don't fall short of your optimal training diet....

> Consume vitamin C-rich foods with non-haem iron sources to optimize absorption.

> Avoid drinking tea with non-haem iron sources, since that would reduce absorption.

> Eat lots of wholemeal bread, eggs, nuts and seeds to ensure sufficient zinc intake.

> Top up omega 3s with linseed, rapeseed oil, walnut and walnut oil and pumpkin seeds.

Vegans

All the above advice applies to vegans, too, although there is the added challenge of achieving a balanced healthy diet without dairy products and eggs. The most important issue of concern is calcium. You'll need to ensure you get sufficient calcium (see page 107) from non-dairy sources or from supplementation. Iron is also in short supply in a vegan diet – consume plenty of fortified breakfast cereals, pulses and green leafy vegetables, and consider having your ferritin and haemoglobin levels assessed by your doctor if you are feeling fatigued or weak and showing pallor. Another micronutrient that you may fall short of is vitamin B12, abundant in milk and dairy products, meat and fish, but also soya products, fortified cereal and yeast extract. A vitamin B complex is recommended.

The low-carb diet

Regardless of its enduring popularity, I would advise you to give the low-carb diet fad a wide berth during your marathon training. Why? Because carbohydrate is the essential runner's fuel – without it, you simply won't perform to the best of your ability. A landmark study in the 1960's demonstrated that people on a low-carb diet who were asked to cycle until exhaustion on an exercise bike managed only one hour, while those on a moderate carbohydrate diet did 115 minutes and those on a high-carb diet clocked 170 minutes. A study from the University of Connecticut also suggests that a high protein diet makes you significantly more dehydrated during exercise than does a normal balanced diet.

why we are here

Running gives your skin a healthy glow by boosting circulation and flushing out toxins, say dermatologists.

crisis
management 6

❖ Running safe

HOW TO MINIMISE THE RISKS OF RUNNING. PERSONAL SAFETY, WILDLIFE, WEATHER....

Overuse injuries aside, running isn't exactly a high-risk sport, but there are a few points regarding personal safety, extreme weather conditions, traffic and wildlife to bear in mind. Here's how to minimise the risks....

Personal safety

As a female runner, I often hear or read that it isn't 'safe' to go running alone, but the solitude factor is so important to me that I'm not willing to do every run with a partner or group. Besides, there isn't always someone available at a convenient time. Male or female, if you do run alone, read the safety guidelines on the following pages...

Safety guidelines for running alone

❖ Don't get lost! Always run in areas that you are familiar with, so you know where to go if you feel ill at ease for any reason. If you do get lost, don't be embarrassed about asking for directions (ideally, ask a passer-by rather than someone in a car). You may feel silly but it's better than running on and ending up in a deserted wasteland or a dodgy estate.

❖ Let someone know where you're going, and when you'll be back. If there's no one home, leave a note, or send a text message to someone.

❖ You could consider carrying a mobile phone in a bum bag, backpack or pocket – today's phones are small and light enough – or take a coin for making a phone call from a public call box, or even jumping on a bus.

❖ Never wear headphones when you're out running. Music might help pass the time on the treadmill but being oblivious to your surroundings out on the roads is unwise – someone could be following you, or you could fail to hear a car or mountain bike approaching.

❖ Run in areas where there are other people – and at times of the day when there are more people around. Avoid poorly lit areas in the evening and early morning. Vary your routes and times.

If you always go the same way, at the same time, it's just possible that someone might take notice of that fact.

- Consider taking a self-defence class to improve your knowledge of what to do, should you ever get attacked.

- Think about investing in a lightweight personal alarm. If the worst should happen, and you were to be attacked, the piercing noise it emits is likely to give you a few more seconds to act before the attacker recovers.

- Carry a slip of paper in your shoe or shorts pocket with your name, telephone number and blood type on, plus any other relevant medical information (allergies, etc.).

Four-legged friends and foes

It is unlikely that you will complete 16 weeks of marathon training without some kind of 'run in' with a dog, or its owner! Even though most dogs are harmless, it can be alarming when one decides to chase you, jump up or bark as you approach. If you are passing a dog that is off its lead, it is advisable to break into a walk, or call out, 'Is he OK with runners?' as you approach. Try to give some warning of your arrival, since surprising the dog (not to mention its owner) is likely to have negative consequences. What if the owner is nowhere to be seen? Give the dog as wide a berth as possible and walk, don't run, past. Don't make eye contact, or attempt to kick out, or throw anything at the dog – say 'NO' or 'DOWN' in a firm, loud voice.

There is a dinky device that might help if you regularly have to pass aggressive dogs or feel nervous about them. It emits an ultrasonic sound that dogs don't like. It's called 'Dog Off' and it also features an ear-piercing personal safety alarm. A good two-in-one investment.

As for the other animals you may encounter while running, since moving to the countryside a couple of years ago, I've been pursued by horses, cows, sheep and even geese on my off-road meanders. If you are running off-road – always follow the Countryside Code, shutting gates, keeping your dog on its lead where specified and respecting rights of way signs. As with dogs, don't surprise livestock, but make some noise, so that they know you are coming. Stick to field borders, rather than going straight across the middle, to avoid alarming them, particularly if you are running with a dog. If large animals – including deer – have young ones, you may have to find a different route altogether. It isn't wise to come between a cow and its calf or to approach a deer with foal.

The runner's Green Cross Code

The golden rule with traffic is to be seen, but never to assume that you have been – even in daylight. Choose running kit in bright colours or with fluorescent panels or strips, and always wear something reflective at night, even if it is simply an armband. If you're running on country roads, face the oncoming traffic unless you are approaching a blind bend, and keep well in. Avoid doing speed work or timed sessions on routes that involve crossing roads or you may be tempted to run out without looking for oncoming traffic. Be particularly vigilant about cars backing out of drives, and pushbikes riding on the pavements.

Ticks

If you are running in long grass or undergrowth, consider wearing long pants rather than shorts, to avoid the risk of getting a tick. These nasty little creatures bury their heads under your skin and feed on your blood – they can also cause Lyme's disease. Always check yourself (and your dog) when you return home for signs of ticks – if you find one, don't pull it straight out but twist it out in an anti-clockwise direction. Special 'tick hooks' are available from vets for tick removal – they work just as well on humans!

Whether the weather is fine or foul...

Feeling hot hot hot!

By far the greatest number of race casualties to be seen in the Flora London Marathon was in 1996, when the midday temperate hit 21 degrees C, which demonstrates how important it is to take a few sensible precautions in hot weather.

- To prevent getting overheated in hot weather, take a dip in a cold bath, the sea or a swimming pool before you begin running. Researchers from Charles Sturt University in Australia found that this enabled exercisers to run four minutes longer on a treadmill than those who did not take the icy plunge.

- Drink more: since you sweat a lot more in hot conditions, you need to drink more fluids to prevent your body from overheating – ensure you do this before, during and after running.

- Consider running very early or late to avoid the heat of the day. In temperatures above 26 degrees C, accompanied by humidity, it is advisable to give running a miss.

- Wear as little as possible – shorts and a vest and a sun visor.

- Sports sunglasses should filter out UVA and UVB rays. Running consistently without protection can increase the risk of glaucoma and cataracts. Go for orange, brown or mirrored lenses to combat glare and bright light.

- Don't forget about sun protection. You need SPF 20 at least, and a sweat-resistant brand. When applying, remember the tops of your ears (your head, if you have a bald spot or thinning hair), the backs of your ankles and sides of your neck.

Baby, it's cold outside

There are bound to be days during your training when the weather is looking less than inviting. That's no reason to stay inside, but you should consider the following points:

- Spend longer warming up in cold weather to prevent muscle tears and strains, and to allow your cardiovascular system to adapt gradually.

- Ensure your trainers have good traction on wet pavements and anywhere icy.

- Eat – don't run on empty. Cold days mean you need to insulate yourself before you set off.

- Wrap up your extremities. In icy weather, blood is shunted to vital areas such as your internal organs, while blood vessels near to the skin surface close to prevent heat loss. Your fingers, toes, ears and nose are vulnerable to frostbite when it's really cold, so wear a hat and mittens or gloves, and perhaps even a scarf.

∴ Keep drinking. The cold weather can fool you into believing you aren't thirsty or sweating much, but you are, so drink plenty.

∴ Avoid speed work that involves lots of rest periods, since you will get cold very quickly. Also, on long runs, beware of going too far, and having to walk a long way home.

∴ To make getting out the door that bit easier, put your clothes on the radiator or in the tumble dryer to make them toasty when you put them on.

∴ Dealing fast and effectively with injuries

According to a report on running injuries published in 1997, 45 to 70 per cent of runners experience some kind of musculoskeletal injury each year. Hopefully, by heeding the advice and following the exercises in the 'body maintenance' section of Chapter 3, and sticking to the realistic and achievable training programmes in this book, you won't suffer the same fate. But no runner is immune to injury, so it is as well to take a look at what to do if you do experience something more than a niggle, and at some of the more common injuries that runners have to contend with. There are two main types of injuries: acute ones, which is when something happens 'suddenly', such as if you fall and twist your ankle; and, more prevalent among runners, 'chronic' or overuse injuries, which come on gradually. Whatever type of injury you have, the first port of call should be to RICE it.

RICE tips

RICE is an acronym for Rest, Ice, Compression and Elevation, the standard protocol that you should follow to minimise pain, swelling and inflammation, and hopefully, reduce the amount of time that you'll be laid off from running.

➣ *Rest* – take a few days off; it's better than pushing through pain and ending up having to take weeks off.

➣ *Ice* – use crushed ice not cubes, or bags of frozen peas or sweetcorn, that can be moulded into shape. Don't put directly onto your skin – it will burn; protect your skin with clingfilm, muslin or a tea towel. Aim for 15 minutes every hour for the first few hours and then 15 minutes every two hours. When I did the Himalayan 100-Mile race my most-cherished possession was my supply of instant cold packs – bags full of crystals with a pouch inside containing a chemical that, when you burst it, makes the crystals turn icy cold. The cool lasts for 30 minutes and then you have to dispose of the bag. Another product, Liquid Ice, is a reusable bandage which is instantly cold when you remove it from its wrapper.

➣ *Compression* – use an elasticated bandage or sleeve to compress the area; this reduces blood flow and swelling. If you don't have one handy use Lycra shorts or running tights.

➣ *Elevation* – if possible, elevate the injured part above your heart.

Sometimes the acronym is extended to RICED, in which D stands for drugs. If your injury is accompanied by swelling, redness and heat, non-steroidal anti-inflammatories, such as ibuprofen or aspirin, can help. Don't start them for 48 hours, and don't use for more than 7 to 10 days. The drug will have done its job by then, and after that it is merely masking the pain. NEVER take drugs to help you train without pain.

See a specialist

If your injury is acute, as soon as possible make an appointment to see a doctor or sports medicine specialist for a proper diagnosis and plan of action. If the injury is chronic, or if the pain comes and goes, use the RICE protocol for 2 to 3 days to see whether this gets rid of it. If not, then waste no more time and get to a specialist.

Make the most of your appointment

When you consult a physiotherapist, or other sports practitioner, ensure that you come away clear about what your problem is, what the likely cause is and what action you need to take, both to hasten recovery and to prevent it happening again. In particular, if you are given exercises or stretches to do, ensure you know exactly how to do them, and how often. Don't beafraid to take notes or ask for diagrams, if it helps. Also get an idea of how long you will be out of running for, and how many appointments the practitioner anticipates that you will need. Be wary if your treatment seems to be going on and on, without any signs of the injury improving. Either they haven't found the true cause, or they are keeping you coming back by withholding either information or treatment. Also, do what you're told! There is no sense in paying good money for expert advice if you don't heed it.

A final thought: half of all injuries are recurring ones, suggesting that the problem usually lies in training errors – doing too much, doing it badly or not allowing enough time to recover. If the same old injury plagues you time and again, it's well worth investing in an appointment with a specialist – a physiotherapist, biomechanist or podiatrist – to determine what's causing it and what can be done to solve it once and for all.

Healing alternatives

- Arnica – available in gel, cream or pill form – is a homeopathic remedy for bruising, and is very effective in reducing inflammation and swelling. A study published in Advances in Therapy found that arnica gel relieved the symptoms of knee pain in osteoarthritis sufferers.
- Avoid alcohol, which will exacerbate inflammation and delay healing by increasing blood flow.
- DON'T apply heat to injuries. You might feel like consoling yourself with a long hot bath but the heat won't help your injury.
- Be positive. Research shows that a positive outlook on recovery can speed up the process.
- A TENS unit can provide relief for chronic or acute pain through electrotherapy, administered via pads that you attach to the appropriate injured site of the body.

The hit list

These are some of the more common injuries that runners encounter. I've included symptoms and risk factors to help you identify what the problem might be. If RICE hasn't helped, get to see a specialist as soon as possible.

Achilles tendinitis

Inflammation of the Achilles tendon along the back of the lower leg.

What it feels like: pain, stiffness and tenderness at the back of the heel, particularly in the morning, when rising onto toes and during running, especially when you start out.

Risk factors: being male, overpronation, tight calf muscles, if female regular wearing of high heels, an excessively stiff forefoot in your running shoe.

Case notes: ask your sports doctor for a programme to regain eccentric calf strength and flexibility.

Iliotibial band syndrome

The iliotibial band is a fibrous band that extends from the hip to just below the knee – it is actually a very long tendon that is attached to the tensor fascia latae muscle in the hip. In iliotibial band syndrome, the band becomes overtight and inflamed, causing it to rub against the surrounding structures. It accounts for 12 per cent of all running injuries.

What it feels like: a sharp pain or friction on the lateral side of the knee, and even a 'catching' sensation as the band slides over the bony prominence of the thigh bone.

Risk factors: inexperience, lots of downhill running, excessive pronation, hip abductor weakness (particular gluteus medius), running on cambered surfaces or frequent athletic track running.

Case notes: do exercises 5 and 8 on pages 51-2 and the Thomas Test stretch on page 54 – religiously.

Ankle sprain

What if feels like: there's a difference between 'turning' your ankle, after which you may be able to continue running, and a full-blown sprain which entails a fully or partially torn ligament, swelling and bruising.

Risk factors: not looking where you are going! Running on uneven ground. Weak ankles.

Case notes: see a doctor to ensure no bones are broken. Do not begin running again until you can move the ankle freely in all directions and hop continuously without pain. A wobble board can help strengthen the muscles of the lower legs and prevent reoccurrence.

Muscle strains and tears

Excessive strain on, or rupture of, muscle fibres. Muscle strains and pulls are most likely to occur in muscles that pass over two joints, such as the upper calf or hamstring. A strain will cause pain, and perhaps tightness and swelling, but doesn't result in a tear of the muscle fibres. A tear usually occurs as a result of a sudden movement in an extreme range, such as during explosive drills or speed work. A tear – either partial or total – is obviously accompanied by sudden pain, and will show as bruising or even a 'trail' of bleeding in the muscle. RICE is the first line of treatment, but get yourself to a specialist quickly if you suspect a tear.

Risk factors: failing to warm-up, previous strain or tear in same area, overtraining, poor flexibility.

Case notes: strains and tears often return, because a build-up of scar tissue hampers smooth muscle contraction, and the pain causes you to alter your biomechanics. Massage can help dissipate scar tissue, while a programme of appropriate stretching and strengthening can prevent reoccurrences.

Piriformis syndrome

The piriformis muscle is a deep hip rotator and plays a very important role in stabilising the pelvis and allowing for correct gait. It can be a little over-sensitive however, and switch off or go into spasm.

What it feels like: piriformis-induced problems are varied, so the symptoms are diverse. A deep, dull ache in the buttock is a common sign, as is a shooting or persistent pain down the hamstring (this is because the sciatic nerve runs close to or through the piriformis muscle).

Risk factors: poor pelvic stability, weak hip abductors or hamstrings, lower back and hip rotator tightness.

Case notes: if the piriformis goes into spasm, a 'trigger release' technique can bring almost instant relief – see a sports massage therapist or physio-therapist. Try the hip rotator stretch on page 53, holding it for up to a minute and then repeating. Lie on top of a tennis ball to work into the painful areas.

Plantar fascitis

Inflammation of the plantar fascia, a sheath of connective tissue that runs along the entire bottom of the foot and fans out to all the toes.

What it feels like: pain under the base of the heel (where the platar fascia originates). It is often at its worst first thing in the morning. If you palpate the heel, you'll probably find an area of acute tenderness.

Risk factors: abnormal running gait, tight deep calf muscles, weak foot muscles, high arches, excessive mileage.

Case notes: ask a physio about exercises to strengthen the 'lumbricals', the deep foot muscles.

Runner's knee

This is generally caused by the kneecap maltracking, causing pain and inflammation and possibly degeneration of the cartilage.

What it feels like: persistent, throbbing or stabbing pain behind the knee cap, a sensation of heat in the joint. Particularly bad on going down or upstairs and on rising from a chair. It is estimated that 60 per cent of knee injuries are a result of the kneecap maltracking (see page 57).

Risk factors: weak vastus medialis muscle (the innermost quadriceps), tight lateral structures around the knee joint, weak pelvic stabilisers, overpronation, flat feet

Case notes: the prone kicking exercise on page 49 can help prevent runner's knee.

Shin problems

They used to be called shin splints, but tibial stress syndrome is the official name for conditions in which there is inflammation of the connective tissue or 'fascia', which attaches to the main shinbone (the tibia).

What it feels like: pain along the front of the shin (anterior tibial stress syndrome), or the inner side of the lower leg (medial tibial stress syndrome), just where the muscle and bone meet. Unlike stress fractures, the exact area of soreness can't be determined – it's a more general tendernesss.

Risk factors: being a beginner, overtraining, overpronation, worn out or inappropriate shoes, imbalance between calves and shin muscles.

Another shin condition, known as compartment syndrome, is characterised by generalised shin pain that always comes on at the exact same time or distance into your run. This is because compartment syndrome is caused by the muscles swelling within the sausage skin-like 'fascia' of the shin, with a resultant increase in pressure to the point at which the structures are pressing against the shin bone and blood flow is compromised. The symptoms include leg pain, unusual nerve sensations (paresthesia) and muscle weakness.

Case notes: also read 'Stress fractures', below, to rule this out. If a compartment syndrome is suspected – see a sports doctor straight away. RICE will not help.

Stress fractures

A stress fracture is a tiny hairline crack in the bone, caused by repeated impact. The most common sites in runners are the shin and bones of the feet.

What it feels like: a very specific point of tenderness upon the bone. An expert may use a vibrating tuning fork to strike the same bone, away from the site of tenderness – if this causes further pain at the hot spot, then this indicates a stress fracture.

Risk factors: training on hard surfaces, building up mileage too quickly, inadequate rest, wearing worn out trainers, excessive pronation, being amenorrhoeic, being an older runner.

Case notes: do not run on a suspected stress fracture – or you may cause a full-blown fracture.

Braces & supports

The trouble with many braces and supports is that the amount of support they provide isn't going to help much if you've got a serious problem, and if you haven't – well, you probably don't need one. While a tubigrip elasticated bandage might keep the muscle warm, it isn't sturdy enough to prevent an injury or change mechanics. More heavy-duty braces, such as knee supports with metal hinges and the like, are more likely to have an impact, but they are expensive and fairly restrictive to wear. Far better to find out from a sports medicine expert what the problem is. There are also occasions where a support could make things worse. If, for example, you have runner's knee, then compressing the patella onto the sore area is only going to make the problem worse.

⁖ Occupational hazards

PREVENTION AND CURE OF COMMON RUNNING AFFLICTIONS AND TROUBLES

Athlete's foot

Athlete's foot is a fungal infection that loves damp, sweaty places, so it isn't any wonder it attacks runners' feet. If you are prone to this painful and itchy condition, try dabbing tea tree oil between your toes after you have thoroughly washed and dried them, and wear flip-flops if you are in public, wet areas, such as shower blocks or gym changing rooms. An attack can be curbed by using an anti-fungal product, such as Lamisil or Daktarin – but remember, your trainers may be harbouring the culprit: soak your trainer insoles in a tea tree oil solution or spray with an anti-fungal spray.

Blisters

Blisters are a build-up of fluid between the upper and lower layers of the skin, caused by friction between you and your shoes or socks. Hardly life-threatening, they can however cause untold misery to runners who are prone to them. If you are one, avoid cotton or seamed socks and ensure your shoes fit perfectly. If you get a blister, protect it from further friction with a blister plaster, moleskin or even surgical tape. You need to pop it only if it feels painful. If you do opt to pop, then use a sterilised needle heated in a flame, and pop it close to the unblistered skin to drain the fluid. Dab antiseptic lotion on and then cover with a blister plaster for at least 48 hours before leaving the area bare. Always have a stash of blister plasters handy. Look for those that create a 'second skin' between the blister and your footwear, such as Compeed or Hydra-Gel, to cushion the skin. These are also breathable and waterproof, so your blister won't fester or get sore.

Black toenails

Black toenails are the result of bruising and blood blisters under the nail, normally caused by your toes repeatedly hitting the front of your shoe. Shoes that are too tight, or too big, can cause this – as can running downhill. If the toenail just looks ugly and doesn't hurt – leave it alone. It will either grow out or, more likely, fall off. If, however, there is a soreness and pressure behind the nail, you may need to drain the blood blister by piercing the nail. A podiatrist or doctor can do this for you or, if you are brave, you can do it yourself, using a sterilised sharp object such as a safety pin. Once the blood has drained, bathe with antiseptic and tape the nail in place.

Cramp

Cramp is an involuntary, sharp contraction of muscle that happens either during or immediately after exercise. The cause of cramping is not well understood – it is often associated with extreme exertion, dehydration and an imbalance of electrolytes. It may also be to do with malfunction in the muscle contraction process due to fatigue. It certainly seems to occur most frequently when fatigued, which is probably why 67 per cent of marathon runners have reported experience of cramp. Cramps most often occur in muscles that span two joints, such as the calf or hamstrings. Research from the University of Cape Town shows that stretching provides almost instant relief for cramp, so try this first. Next ask yourself whether you have been drinking enough (if you've had around 220 ml every 15 to 20 minutes, you should be fine), and then, what have you been drinking? If the answer is water, try switching to sports drink, to replace sodium and potassium. If you are regularly afflicted by cramp, ensure you are getting sufficient calcium, too, since this has a major role to play in muscular contraction.

Rashes

A sweat rash under your arms, under the breasts or in the groin area is an unpleasant, but surprisingly common, running affliction. Minimise the risk by always showering immediately after running, not wearing dirty kit, and by using petroleum jelly to prevent chafing. If you do get a rash, treat it with an anti-fungal lotion or cream – preferably one combined with hydrocortisone – to reduce redness and itching.

Stitches

Most runners get a stitch at some point during training or racing, but still we don't really know what causes them. The latest theories relate to the diaphragm muscle becoming fatigued, rather than irritated by the jolting movement of running, as formerly thought. Regardless of the cause, researchers from the University of Newcastle in Australia suggest avoiding big meals prior to running, particularly foods high in fat and sugar, and to warm up thoroughly. You may find that changing the rhythm of your breathing to match your footfall helps, but in my experience, walking for a few moments while kneading the painful area is the simplest solution.

Tummy trouble

Half of all runners experience some kind of bowel or stomach problem during training or racing, whether it is abdominal pain, heartburn, nausea, diarrhoea or sickness. Among the many and varied possible causes are dehydration, sensitivity to a particular food, reduced blood flow to the intestines (perhaps due to eating too close to running) and the jolting action of running. If you can identify what caused your tummy trouble, so much the better – avoid the trigger when important training runs or races are approaching. If, however, you aren't sure what's causing the problem, consider the following common irritants:

- Caffeine – can irritate the gastrointestinal tract (which is why it often makes us 'go' in the morning).

- Sugar – highly concentrated sugar solutions – such a sports drinks – can cause GI distress in some people. That's why it's vital that you experiment with sports drinks, in different concentrations in training to see what works for you.

- Fibrous foods – prior to a race or training run is the rare time when you don't want to opt for fibrous foods, since they take a long time to digest and absorb a lot of water, making you feel bloated and heavy.

> Dairy products – some people find dairy products hard to digest.

> Fruit – can cause stomach cramping.

> Asprin and ibuprofen – non-steroidal anti-inflammatories can cause stomach upsets and even bleeding if taken too often, or on an empty stomach.

The Last Resort

A SURVIVAL STRATEGY FOR COMPLETING THE RACE WHEN TRAINING HASN'T GONE TO PLAN

You may have been struck down with flu for a month, you may have been given a huge project with a hideous deadline at work, you may simply have failed to pull your finger out – whatever the reason, you haven't managed to get the training in, and you are now wondering whether you can make it to the finish line.

Well, you have two options. You pull out of the race, and perhaps defer your entry to next year (not all races will allow this), or you read on to find out about the last resort.

The 'last resort' is a walk-run program that should get you round in one piece, if not, perhaps, as fast as you had first envisaged. Having said that, many people have successfully used a walk-run strategy to help them improve their finish time, not just get round the course. According to Jeff Galloway, a leading proponent of the walk-run protocol, the average improvement made by veteran marathon runners who adopted the strategy instead of running continuously was 13 minutes. 'Mentally, [the walk-run sessions] are a way to break up the marathon into segments that are doable,' he says. 'Physically, they allow the muscles to recover before they hit the wall.' Galloway also insists that many sub-three-hour runners have successfully used a walk-run race plan.

Rule 1: walk-run from mile one. Not from when your legs begin to feel a bit tired, but from the very beginning. What should the breakdown of walking and running be? It depends on how far you progressed with your long runs. If you didn't make it beyond 13 miles, then walk for 1 minute after every 5 minutes of running at your Level 2 pace. If you got closer to 17-18 miles, I suggest running at your Level 2 pace until you hit each mile marker. Then walk for one minute. If you feel self-conscious about walking, particularly in the early stages of the race, pretend to be adjusting your race number, taking a drink or stretching. Ignore spectators urging you to get running again! 'The most important walk breaks are the early ones,' says Galloway. If you feel absolutely great by mile 22, then you could risk cutting the walk breaks to 30 seconds, or even doing away with them altogether; but DON'T be tempted to do this earlier in the race.

Rule 2: try to practise your walk-run protocol at least a few times in training before race day, to get an idea of how it feels, and to determine your exact walk-run breakdown.

Rule 3: use sports drink instead of water to rehydrate. Not only because it will provide you with extra energy, but because you are more at risk of hyponatremia at a very slow pace and the salts contained within an isotonic drink will prevent it.

Rule 4: remember your body scan. Don't be afraid to stop and stretch out anything that feels tight or tense – you aren't racing the clock now.

Rule 5: read the mental strategies on pages 89–91 to help your brain get you round the course, and remember to check out the race tactics on pages 144–5.

Rule 6: this is a last resort strategy – but it isn't infallible; if you are feeling really terrible on the way round, you may have to consider dropping out.

countdown to race day 7

:: Preparing for the big day

GETTING THE PRACTICAL STUFF RIGHT

At least a few weeks before race day, you should receive final instructions from the race organisers, telling you essential things like what to do with your bags, where to pick up your race number (if it hasn't already been sent out to you), how to get to the start line, and including a route map of the course. Carefully read everything you are sent, when you first receive it, and again a week before, and then the day before. There may be little points that you don't take in when the race seems a while off that suddenly become very important the night before. For example, how to attach your ChampionChip to your shoe, or what colour balloons to look for at the start area for the appropriate start pen....

A room for the night

If you are on a 'race package' in which your accommodation is booked for you and transport to the start is included, that's two things less to worry about; if not, you'll need to book somewhere in advance. If it's a big race, such as the Flora London marathon, you'll need to book a good while in advance, and then plan your travel arrangements to the start (and from the finish area).

Some race information leaflets will suggest places for runners to stay – and these places may even provide transport to the start. If not, here are some questions to ask your potential hotelier/guest house provider:

:: Is it quiet at night?

:: Will I be able to get a suitable meal (a carbohydrate-based meal such as pasta, rice or potatoes – but perhaps give the curry a miss) at the hotel or close-by?

:: How close is it to the start area and how would I get there from the hotel?

:: Will you be able to serve me breakfast early (you'll need to eat at least two hours before the start time, preferably three hours).

:: Will you be able to provide me with something appropriate for breakfast? (a whopping fry-up is out of the question!).

If you aren't staying away from home the night before the race, and have a journey to contend with in the morning, it's even more important that you have your route well planned. Are you sure you can park there, or, if you're travelling on public transport, will you definitely be able to get a taxi from the station or depot to the start area? Remember that access roads may be closed. Allow plenty of time for unexpected traffic, getting lost, train delays or, the worst of all eventualities, breaking down.

Get familiar

You should be able to see a map of the course either in the race literature or on the Internet. Study it properly – don't just glance at it. Where are the hills? What landmarks are there that you can set in your mind and keep an eye out for? Where are your supporters going to stand? How will they get to that point, and from there to the next vantage spot? Remember to say which side of the road you want your fans to stand on – be very specific, and ensure they also have a copy of the route map.

If at all feasible, try driving or cycling the marathon course so that you are aware of what's in store. Try running some of it, too, perhaps the last few miles, so that you can practise visualising the finish and yourself running strongly towards it. However, don't do this the night before the race, when you should be resting, and when it may serve to make you anxious rather than more prepared.

What to pack

What you need to take with you is obviously an individual decision, and depends on where you are going, how long for and whether you'll be staying on. Let's look at some of the less obvious things you might need....

- A local road atlas of the place where you're headed, in case you have trouble finding the start area.

- Nail scissors. Cut your toenails straight across and shorter than the tips of your toes to avoid them ending up black and bruised.

- Mobile phone and charger – you may need it to help you find relatives and friends at the finish area. (If you are going abroad, remember to let your phone company know at least 24 hours in advance, to check that you can access the usual services, and to take an adaptor plug.)

- Surgical tape to tape down shoelaces that have a tendency to come undone, and to tape up vulnerable areas of your feet, to prevent blisters.

- A basic first aid kit: immodium for upset tummies, ibuprofen or another NSAID for any muscular aches or pains, blister plasters, petroleum jelly.

- A relaxing, soothing aromatherapy oil for the post-race bath.

- Hair ties or sweatbands for long hair.

- Any 'special' foods or drinks that you might want for before, during and after the race.

Kit to go

Even if it's been grey and miserable for weeks – or relentless sunshine – you should pack different kit options for different weathers – you just never know. Don't forget seasonal extras such as sunglasses, sun screen and a visor – or gloves and a hat for cooler climes. The checklist below isn't exhaustive, but will help you think about what you need. It's a good idea to put all your kit on before you pack it to ensure you haven't forgotten something essential, like your race socks or sports bra. For more vocal support on the way round the course, write or stitch your name onto the back and front of your race vest or T-shirt. It gives spectators something to shout out and you'll be amazed how encouraging it is to hear your name being called.

Kit checklist

- Running shoes and spare laces
- Running socks
- Comfortable underwear
- Shorts or bottoms
- Sports bra
- Vest or t-shirt
- Waterproof top (gilet or sleeved, depending on what you are used to)
- Bin liner and disposable warm clothes, hat and gloves for start line.

:• Winding down

WHY, HOW AND WHEN TO TAPER YOUR TRAINING FOR BEST RESULTS ON RACE DAY

With three weeks to go until the marathon, you may feel this is your chance to get in some decent training. Wrong! This is the time to start winding your training down. Performing well on marathon day isn't just a matter of peaking in your fitness, it's also about ensuring you are fully recovered from the rigours of training, so that you can do your best and feel fresh and ready on the day. Now is the perfect time to devise your race strategy, since you will have a good idea of your capabilities and aspirations.

Devising your race plan

'Get to the finish line in one piece' does not constitute a race strategy. You must stand on the start line with a target finish time in mind, and an idea of your 'split times'. Split times are simply the amount of time it takes you to complete any given section of the course – it could be each mile or kilometre, every 10 km, or the first and second half of the race.

Look closely at the times and speeds you have accomplishing in your training. If, for example, you find that you have run 18 miles at a speed of 9 minutes per mile in your training (and felt shattered afterwards), let's face it, it is unlikely that you'll be able to run a further 8 miles at the same speed on race day. But slowing your pace by an extra 30 to 60 seconds a mile will make the race far more comfortable, and your likelihood of success far greater. If this is your first marathon, be conservative in your target – the idea is to complete, not compete.

Once you have established your target time, calculate what speeds you should run at to get consistent split times for each mile, and when the start gun sounds try to achieve this pace immediately – your goal should be to try to run the 26th mile at the same pace as the 1st! Haile Gebrselassie broke the 10 km world record by varying his pace by less than one second per lap for 23 of the 25 laps – he even sped up on the last two. Of course, he didn't have thousands of other runners jostling for space with him in the opening kilometres, which is why marathoners often aim for a 'negative split', in which you run the second half of the race slightly faster than the first half. Whether you go for a negative split or even splits, you certainly don't want to be slowing down as the miles pass.

Doing the splits

Simply convert your target time to minutes, then divide by 26.2. You'll end up with a 'decimal' number, which you then need to convert to minutes and seconds to give you a split time for each mile.

Example

Target time: 3 hr 40 min = 220 min
220 divided by 26.2 = 8.40
8.40 = 8 min 24 sec per mile

The next stage is to work out the accumulative time for each mile.

Example

8 min 24 sec per mile means that at mile 3,
your watch should read 25.12

Take your split times with you on race day. One option is to write the mile times on a piece of card, or even on your arm, or upside down on your race number, or on a wristband, so that you have a permanent reminder as you run the course. Alternatively, work out and memorise your splits for larger chunks of the race, say, each quarter. This is simpler, but poses the risk of your going too fast or slow at a crucial stage. Whichever strategy you choose, stick with it and make the necessary adjustments to your pace if you aren't running to plan.

Pace groups

A common feature of larger and big city marathons these days are 'pace groups'. These are set up with 'leaders' whose role is to run the race at a constant pace to achieve a set time – say, 4 hours. Pacers are normally advertised well in advance of the race, so check the pre-race details to see if they will be present at your marathon, and where to find them at the start. There's no obligation to stay in the group just because you start with them – equally, there's no guarantee that the leaders will get things right: they are only human like the rest of us, and could easily have a bad day.

The taper caper

As you now know, running overload causes muscle damage, to which the body has to adapt. It also expends energy, and depletes carbohydrate stores in muscle. To maximise your recovery and optimise the chances of a great race, you need to give the body plenty of time to repair the muscle damage, replenish carbohydrate stores and rest weary limbs. The decrease in training volume leading up to a big event is called the taper. A proper taper will give you some mental drive, too, so that you line up at the start feeling raring to go.

How to taper

As you will have seen in the 16-week programmes, the last long run takes place three weeks before the day; after that run training volume is steadily reduced. Research undertaken at Ball State University suggests this is the optimum amount of time between the last hard effort and the race itself. Don't be tempted to squeeze in another long run the following weekend.

While you could be forgiven for worrying that you will 'lose' your fitness during the taper, remember that many of the adaptations that have taken place are fairly enduring changes, such as the number and size of mitochondria in the muscle cells, an increased number of red blood cells, and stronger muscle fibres. Research shows that, by reducing your training volume to a third of your highest level, you would be able to maintain your cardiovascular fitness for around eight weeks – so don't worry about a mere three weeks causing a decline in your potential. What's more important to consider is that there is very little to be gained in the way of endurance, speed or strength now.

It is not unusual to feel suddenly lethargic and heavy during the taper. This is partly because your glycogen stores are full (since you aren't continually depleting them with training), and each gram of glycogen stores with it 3 grams of water. Your body has also become accustomed to a large volume of activity, and removing this from the equation can leave you feeling as if you could barely run a mile, let alone a marathon. Don't see this as a sign to go out for a gruelling training run; simply ensure that you aren't overeating and that you are well hydrated, and try some strides to wake your legs up. The last two weeks of training include shorter runs and a few pacier sessions to keep you ticking over. Sticking to grass and softer surfaces will reduce impact and muscle damage, but be extra careful on uneven ground.

A sports massage in the final week (perhaps after your run the week before the marathon) can help alleviate any tightness and encourage blood flow and recovery in the muscles. Don't leave it to the day before, though, since it may leave you feeling low on energy, and don't have one if you have never had one before. Remember the rule – never try anything new at this late stage of the game.

Try to get plenty of rest during the last few days, too. Avoid spending more time than you have to on your feet, or engage in tiring activities such as gardening or DIY. Even if you don't sleep well the night before, you will be fine so long as you are well rested in the lead up to the event.

Adjusting your diet

Another point to watch for in these final weeks is your food and fluid intake. You will have become accustomed to eating more than usual but, now that you are not training so much, you need to make sure you don't take too many calories on board. And, because of the importance of carbohydrate to your running performance, you need to maximise your glycogen stores by concentrating on a carbohydrate-focused diet. Aim for 5 to 7 g of carbohydrate for every

kg of your body weight (for example, if you weigh 70 kg, that's 350 to 490 g per day). That doesn't mean you need to eat pasta for breakfast lunch and dinner, but it does mean that you should ensure you have carbohydrate at every meal…. Equally, remember that carbohydrate means cereal, pasta, potatoes, rice, bread products, bananas, dried fruit and starchy vegetables – not pastries, biscuits, cakes, pizza, flapjacks and crisps!

It's a great idea to try a 'mealtime race rehearsal' – in other words, have your pre-race supper (see overleaf) the night before, and your pre-race breakfast the morning before one of your final training runs, to see that it all feels comfortable and nothing repeats on you or causes gastrointestinal distress.

Carbo-load wisely

Carbo-loading is one of those phrases that has made its way into the public domain, but what does it really mean? Well, the original strategy was to deplete glycogen stores by cutting out carbohydrate from the diet (and running) for 3 to 4 days. Then, a few days before a race, you would pile in the carbs, in the hope that your 'hungry' glycogen stores would snap it all up and overcompensate by taking on more than they would have done previously. However, recent research has shown that simply increasing carbohydrate intake for three days prior to a race, while simultaneously reducing mileage (which is exactly what you do in the lead-up to a race) has an equally beneficial effect on glycogen storage volume.

Research suggests that plenty of vitamin E and C in the weeks prior to the race will reduce muscle damage and aid recovery. Step up your intake of vitamin C and E rich fruits and vegetables, or consider taking a supplement as race day approaches.

The final 24 hours

You may well be spending much of this day travelling. If not, then make the most of it and relax. Get out some uplifting videos and relax in front of the TV with a big bottle of water, read an absorbing book or go for a gentle stroll in the fresh air. This is also the ideal time to do your final check of all your kit and race instructions and revisit the mental strategies on page 91.

Don't be afraid to have the odd cup of tea and coffee if you usually do, but don't overdo it, and avoid eating or drinking anything that you are not used to.

Although in theory you ought to go to bed early to get plenty of rest, many people end up lying in bed thinking about the day ahead. Don't get stressed if you find yourself wide awake at 3 o'clock in the morning – it's your muscles, not your brain, that benefit most from sleep and you'll still be able to run well even if you have spent most of the night staring at the bedroom ceiling! A milky drink before bed and a warm (not hot) bath may help you relax and feel sleepy enough for bed. Interestingly, a study by the Social Research Issues Centre in Oxford found that runners in the Flora London Marathon who had sex the night before ran, on average, five minutes faster than those who abstained. The researchers weren't sure why, but there's a good chance that it could help to dispel pre-race tension and aid sleep.

The last supper

A lot of emphasis is placed on the 'last supper', what with pasta parties and carbo-loading strategies, but ideally the largest meal on the eve of race day should be eaten earlier in the day, and just a light snack taken in the evening. Why? Well, a heavy meal won't help you sleep well, and it may also mean you wake up feeling sluggish. If you don't fancy a big lunch – or can't practically arrange to eat at lunchtime, at least have your evening meal early to allow plenty of time to digest the food. Talking of digestion, there is more information on gastric upsets on page 121, but you may want to avoid gas-producing foods in your last pre-race meals – such as cabbage, Brussels sprouts, beans, pulses and high-fibre cereals. Drinking alcohol isn't advisable the night before your marathon, but one glass of wine or beer shouldn't hurt if it will help you to relax. Remember to balance it out with lots of other non-alcoholic fluids, too. Finally, don't go to bed feeling hungry. If you're peckish, have some toast or cereal to take the edge off.

why *we are here*

Regular runners have a lifetime heart attack mortality risk some 70 per cent lower than sedentary people. Studies have shown the heart attack risk in a marathon is 1 in 54,000.

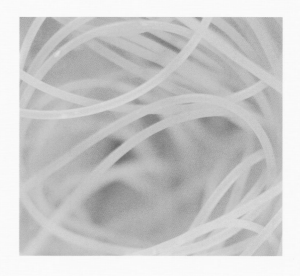

⋮> Seeing success

MENTAL STRATEGIES TO GET YOU IN THE RIGHT FRAME OF MIND

With race day fast approaching, you may suddenly be feeling as if your stomach is tying itself in knots, or doubting whether you really can achieve this goal of yours. Don't worry – these feelings are normal, and they can be used to your advantage, to get you into the right state of readiness for the race, what sport psychologists call your 'zone of optimal functioning'.

Psyching up – or chilling out

When we talk about stress we normally mean it in a negative way, but stress, physiologically speaking, isn't necessarily a bad thing: it's simply our body's way of preparing to deal with an oncoming challenge or situation.

What is more relevant, in performance terms, is the *level* of stress, or what sport psychologists call 'arousal', that you experience prior to performance. The signs of arousal are both physiological and psychological: the former signs include raised heart rate, muscle tension, breathing rate, blood pressure, palm sweating, 'butterflies' and general sweating. Psychological telltale signs are feelings of anxiety, fear and self-doubt. You often hear people talking about getting psyched up to perform, but there's a fine line between being primed for performance and being too hyper to focus properly. The ideal level of arousal differs from person to person, and it's important that you learn what your ideal level is, so that you can prepare adequately for your marathon. Some runners will thrive on the tension that builds before a big race while others will be in and out of the loo, their stomachs in knots. So what about you? Do you like to get pepped up to perform, or do you feel the need to remain calm and keep a hold on your nerves?

One of the best ways to determine which sounds like you is to look back to how you felt prior to other big events in your life. Ideally, these would be other races, but anything that presented a big challenge will do. Did you feel like sitting on your own, collecting your thoughts, or did you want to tear the phone book in half and let out an animal roar? These are all signs that indicate whether you need to look at psyching up, or chilling out.... Once you've decided which is you, follow the guidelines suggested to find some useful strategies that should help get you into the zone.

Me, nervous?

Here are some of the less obvious signs of anxiety and stress....

- **Feelings of fatigue**
- **Flushed skin**
- **Yawning**
- **Voice distortion**
- **Desire to urinate**
- **Cotton feeling in mouth**
- **Trembling muscles/muscular tension.**

Strategies to psyche up

Play it again

Before a training run or race, listen to tunes that fire you up. Research by sport psychologists at Brunel University found that music that moves you will positively affect your mood, elevate your heart rate and reduce anxiety. Ideally, music should match the heart rate at which you plan to work, give or take a few beats. The songs should make you feel good and increase your energy levels – so don't just pick something with 155 bpm that you actually detest, like the latest thrash metal. You may want to listen to music on your way to the race, or take a personal stereo along and listen to it while you warm up and wait for the off.

Activate!

Self-activation is an umbrella term that covers all manner of weird and wonderful ways athletes psyche themselves up. Tennis player Jimmy Connors used to slap himself on the thigh prior to a match; many athletes make use of the crowd, encouraging them to make a noise and get excited, in order to get themselves in the right state of mind. While you might have trouble with the latter strategy ('who's that nutter shouting at us over there?'), bantering with club mates, playing with your dog or kids or firing off some brisk 'strides' might help.

Make a picture

Visualization can be a great way of priming yourself for a race or training run. Use your visualization skills to create a picture of yourself running comfortably and steadily – passing those who set off too fast and are now tiring. Feel how ready your muscles are for the challenge, how your feet are itching to get moving, your heart rate already elevating in anticipation.

Strategies to chill out

Say Om

Learning to meditate can be a very valuable tool in your marathon survival kit. By focusing on a single thought, sound or object, or simply your breathing, you will be able to quieten your mind and switch off from niggling worries and fears. Research shows that meditation can alter the pattern of alpha waves in the brain and invoke a relaxation response. There are many different types of meditation, including transcendental meditation, in which you have your own personal mantra to focus upon.

Take a breather

Utilising a longer exhalation than the length of the inhalation induces a feeling of calm. Breathe in for count of four, allowing the abdomen to swell as your diaphragm rises. Hold for a count of four, then exhale for a count of six, pulling belly button to spine as you expel the air slowly.

Tune in

Music that you find calming and soothing can help you relax before a race. Brunel University researchers found that Japanese classical music increased alpha activity in the brain, associated with relaxation. It doesn't have to be classical, but if you're opting for folk or love songs, make sure that the music you select doesn't have any negative connotations.

Reframe the situation

What we perceive of a situation and the reality are often very different. Imagine, for example, that you are scared of house spiders, and there is one on the bedroom wall. While the objective situation is that there is a small, harmless creature in your bedroom, your perception is likely to engender nothing but fear, anxiety and revulsion. However, the process of cognitive restructuring is used to 'reframe' the situation in a more positive light. Here's an example that might relate to your race day nerves. You are lining up for the race, and your heart's racing, your tummy tumbling and your skin tingling – the accompanying thought might be, 'God, I'm nervous.' This could be restructured as, 'All my body's signals say it's raring to go. I am ready to perform.'

Give yourself a talking to

'I'll never make it. What if I get a stitch? I bet I hit the wall and have to drop out or walk the rest of the way....' Sound familiar? These are some classic examples of negative self-talk. You might think talk is cheap but there's a lot of evidence that the way you talk to yourself has a profound effect on your self esteem and confidence, and can influence your behaviour. Positive self-talk is associated with improved performance while negative self-talk can be detrimental. Your subconscious is listening.... Don't forget about your mantras (page 91).

Pre-performance rituals

There's a lot of research to suggest that mental state prior to performance affects mental state during performance – so it's essential to go into your race with the right mindset. While the psyching up and chilling out strategies will certainly help you achieve this, creating a 'pre-performance ritual' for yourself is a highly effective way of priming you for the race.

A pre-performance ritual is simply a routine that you practise in training, and always do before a race. Once the pre-performance ritual is complete, it acts as a mental 'trigger' that tells you, 'OK, time to perform.' Pre-performance rituals practised by sports stars are as diverse and numerous as the athletes themselves, and there is no point in copying what someone else does. Experiment with a few different strategies along the way but ensure that you end up with an easy-to-follow, consistent routine. My pre-race ritual is a warm-up jog followed by six Sun

Salutations, a sequence of yoga postures. Then I check my shoelaces and I'm all set.

Another great way to get geared up is to create a Circle of Excellence. This is a technique derived from NLP – neurolinguisitic programming – and its purpose is to create a 'virtual toolbag' of all the positive resources you may need for your marathon. For example, let's say you feel you need confidence, determination, discipline and focus. Start by drawing an imaginary circle on the floor (big enough to stand on). Stand close by, and think back to a situation when you felt totally confident. Remember, using all your senses, what it felt like. As soon as you can feel it, step into your circle to deposit it there, stepping out again as the feeling fades. Repeat this sequence with the other attributes you need until you have all your required resources in the circle. Then simply 'pack your circle' away in your pocket, behind your ear, or under your wrist band, until the big day, when you will unpack it and step inside, until you are glowing with excellence....

why we are here

Running makes you more stress-resilient. Volunteers subjected to extreme cold, excessive noise or unpleasant pictures got less stressed by the experience after they had been running, than they did after sitting quietly.

Tips

'In the last two or three days visualize yourself at various points in the race – particularly focus on crossing the finish line. When I won the London Marathon I found myself daydreaming on the last few long runs of pulling away from the pack and crossing the line with my arms raised. On the day it worked out just like that and I had the confidence to make my move 4 miles from the end because I really believed I could win'

– Mike Gratton, winner of the London Marathon, 1983.

{ *Performing well on marathon day isn't just a matter of peaking in your fitness*

❖ Race day: the practicals

LAST MINUTE PREPARATION AND CONSIDERATIONS

What will probably be one of the most memorable days of your life – one way or another – has finally arrived. The key to making it memorable in a good way is to be meticulously prepared, both mentally and physically, and to have the common sense to be flexible enough to adapt your plans. Preparing properly means adopting a strategy for the day – not just the race – so that you can approach your marathon with quiet confidence.

Breakfast time

Research suggests that eating 2 to 4 hours before you run gives you the best chance of topping up fuel stores without causing gastrointestinal discomfort. It's down to personal taste, but make sure you've given this important final meal a try in your race rehearsal. The ideal pre-race meal should include a little fat and protein and a lot of carbohydrate. It could be breakfast cereal with milk, toast with scrambled or boiled egg, or a bagel with peanut butter and banana. Avoid high-fibre foods and dairy products if you are susceptible to tummy upsets. If you usually have a cup or two of tea or coffee in the morning, by all means have one.

What if you feel too nervous to eat?

It really is advisable to eat something; you need to top up the calories your body has burned through sleeping. In a study on cyclists, a 400-calorie breakfast 3 hours before a ride to fatigue enabled them to go for an average of 27 minutes longer than when they just had water. If you can't face solids, then have a liquid breakfast – an energy drink that you are familiar with, or even a meal replacement such as a SlimFast.

What to wear

There isn't anything magical about race kit – it's simply the training kit that you feel most comfortable and happy in, and that suits the conditions you'll be racing in. Take a close look at the weather forecast for race day, and plan accordingly, but have contingency kit for all weather options – you never know what might happen on the day. If it's a morning race, the start is almost certainly going to be during the coolest part of the day. The ubiquitous dustbin liner, with holes cut in for your head and arms, will help conserve body heat and keep light rain off, too. It can easily be discarded once the race is under way.

Even if race morning is a little chilly, don't be tempted to wear too much clothing – you'll be out there a long time, and the chances are that the temperature will increase as the day progresses – not to mention your own body temperature, which will rise as you get into your stride.

Kitbag checklist

Once you leave your accommodation (or home) there's no going back for things you've forgotten. Hopefully, you are already well organised by this point, but scan the checklist on page 127 to ensure you have everything you need to wear. Then look at the items below to see whether any of them seem worth taking.

Sunscreen – Even if it's not clear skies and sunshine, consider protecting your skin.

Sunglasses – Not just to shield your eyes from the sun but to keep out grit and flies, and to give you 'anonymity' and an internal focus.

Tissues – If you get caught short and need to make a pitstop, don't expect the toilets (if there are any) to be fully equipped. It's useful to have your own.

Money – Since you are separated from all your possessions for the duration of the race, it can be useful to have a money note tucked in your sock or in your shorts pocket for eventualities, such as a taxi, if you fail to meet up with your friends and family at the finish for some reason, or for phone calls, food and drink.

Petroleum jelly – smearing it liberally onto all moving parts is one of the best ways of avoiding chafing and soreness, such as jogger's nipple or raw inner thighs.

Blister plasters – If you are susceptible to blisters, you might want to go forearmed with a blister plaster or two in your pocket.

Race number and safety pins – no number, no race!

Split times – written on your race number (upside down of course), on your forearm or on a card that slips inside a wrist band.

Drinks bottle – you don't have to take one, since there will be regular drinks stations en route, but you may prefer to carry your own.

Fuel – in the form of energy drinks, gels or bars, or energy-packed sweets such as jelly babies.

Tips

In the 24 hours before the race I have a standard ritual. Getting everything right on the day can be the difference between a good and a bad race. I have pasta salad and bread for dinner and toast and honey for breakfast. I feel quite calm on race morning, but my nerves are usually terrible the night before, so I acknowledge that and know I'll feel OK the next day.

– Mark Steinle
top male British marathoner

⫶ Race day: on the run

MAKING IT SUCCESSFULLY TO THE START LINE – AND THE FINISH LINE

At the start

Once you've made it to the start area, you've probably got time to kill – you'll need to drop off your baggage, make final kit choices, visit the loo and warm up. The order in which you do these things depends on whether you are alone, your frame of mind and what the weather is like (you don't want to be standing around shivering in your race kit, for example). Don't warm up too long before the race begins or you'll only

get cold again. You don't need to do much in the way of warming up anyway, as it isn't as if you are going to set off at top speed. And since the first mile is likely to be slow (at least in mass participation events) you can use that time to gradually pick up the pace. Walk and jog for 5 to 10 minutes as a warm-up and then do some stretching and mobilisations. You may also want to do a few strides, but don't overdo either the speed or number of these.

On your marks

⠶ Get into your start area with plenty of time to spare and keep moving to avoid getting cold or stiff.

⠶ Be prepared to take a few minutes to cross the start line if you are taking part in one of the big city marathons. Don't panic about time ticking away, and only start your watch when you cross the line.

⠶ Be vigilant about other runners and the myriad clothing, binliners and fluid containers that inevitably litter the ground.

⠶ Check your shoelaces.

⠶ Check that your stopwatch is ready for the off, and remember to start it when you begin running!

⠶ Chat to other runners if it helps you relax, or focus internally if you find that more calming.

⠶ One final tip: ENJOY YOURSELF! There will never be another first marathon for you, so enjoy it to the max. Don't be too hung up over your finish time (whatever it is,it will be a PB!), and soak up the atmosphere and the sense of achievement as much as possible.

Missing 'the wall'

'The wall' is talked of only in hushed tones in running circles, and is as surrounded by mystery as its opposite, the runner's high. So what is 'the wall', and how can you avoid crashing headlong into it?

A brief explanation of the way we use energy during a marathon should help explain the phenomenon. As we've already learned, carbohydrate is stored in the muscle and liver as a substance called glycogen, the quantities of which are limited to only about two hours of steady exercise. Scientists have shown that the faster you run, the quicker your glycogen stores are depleted, while fat reserves remain virtually untouched. On the face of it, this doesn't make sense

– we've got huge reserves of energy stored as fat, yet we prefer to use carbohydrate for all but the easiest forms of exercise. The trouble is, at any slightly harder effort level, fat is a very inefficient source of energy – there needs to be far more oxygen in the muscle for energy to be released than there does from carbohydrate.

So if you've set off too fast – perhaps carried away by the euphoria of the day, or simply through nerves – you'll be burning a high rate of carbohydrate right from the start. If this continues, you'll probably start to run out of carbohydrate at 16 to 20 miles, since there simply isn't enough glycogen to keep you going any longer. When this happens, you'll have to rely almost exclusively on fat, but because fat is such an inefficient fuel, you'll be yielding less energy, and consequently will have no option other than to slow down.

So this is 'the wall' – the point where carbohydrate stores are depleted, and the body has to make the transition to its abundant, but less efficient, fat stores to draw energy. Its effects are likely to be much worse if you have become dehydrated during the run. Sufferers have likened hitting the wall to running through mud, or having concrete blocks tied to their feet. In its worst form, it is accompanied by nausea, mental disorientation and dizziness, too. Is it inevitable? Absolutely not! With forethought, good training and diet, and a sound race plan, which includes realistic split times, regular refuelling and some of the tactics suggested below, you can break through the wall with ease.

Running wisely

Marathon running isn't a sport readily associated with tactics, but there are a number of simple things you can do that will go some way to helping you through the distance.

> A study by scientists at Manchester Metropolitan University found that, in two Olympic Finals, the winner was not the athlete who ran at the fastest speed! He was, in fact, the athlete who had combined a fast speed with the optimal route around the track, avoiding the outside of the bends and running in a straight line wherever possible. In many bigger marathons, the optimum route from start to finish is marked by a line on the road – follow this if you can and you'll be guaranteed not to run further than 26.2 miles!

> On a windy day, think about using other runners for shelter, in a similar way to the 'drafting' strategy that is adopted frequently in cycling. Overcoming a headwind uses 3 to 9 per cent more energy than running on a still day.

> When the going gets tough, instead of worrying about the finish line and whether you'll ever get there, focus on the process of running and each step that needs to be taken to get to the end. Repeat your mantra – a key word or phrase on which to focus, to prevent negative stuff slipping in.

> If the temperature is high, and the sun is shining, head for the shadier, cooler parts of the course wherever possible – overheating and dehydration are pitfalls you want to avoid. But be careful when you pour that cup of water over your head to cool off – if you get wet socks and shoes, you are doomed to suffer blisters!

> Sprinkle a few drops of peppermint oil on a hankie or on the bottom of your running vest and inhale when you feel tired to boost endurance. It might sound crazy but research reported in the *Journal of Sport and Exercise Psychology* found it works!

> If you want to avoid the inglorious spectacle of taking a tumble, be aware of your position and that of others in the race. Don't cut across other runners to get to a drinks station or wave to your friends, or you may end up tripping, or at least be the butt of angry recriminations.

> Tie long hair back! Experiments in wind tunnels have shown that improving your aerodynamics, by tying back or cutting your hair, and wearing more streamlined clothes, can reduce the effects of wind resistance by up to 6 per cent.

> Keep your head up. Not only will it maintain good form and technique, it will also enable you to make eye contact with other runners and spectators and give a confident stance rather than one that looks as if you're slowly wearing yourself into the ground.

Fuel on the run – what, when and how much?

It used to be illegal to drink during a marathon race – now, the medical profession is somewhat wiser and recommends that every runner should drink regularly throughout. Even a 2 per cent level of dehydration can reduce performance by as much as 5 per cent, so drinking correctly is as important to getting a good time as it is to safeguarding your health.

As you approach a drinks station, try to make eye contact with someone holding a drink out so that they know you are going to take it from them. This saves you missing out, or having a drink extended in front of you that ends up down your T-shirt. Some runners can drink and run at the same time – there's a bit of a knack to it that involves taking sips while 'closing' the epiglottis, before allowing the liquid to go down the throat. Others prefer to slow to a walk – or even stop – to prevent a choking fit, and to ensure they actually get some of the liquid down their gullet! If you are going to stop to drink, don't park yourself in front of the drinks station itself, but move on and stand to the side.

Water or sports drink?

The research certainly falls in favour of sports drinks when looking at an endurance event as long as the marathon. However, not everyone can stomach them, and water is a perfectly good way of rehydrating, although it doesn't provide any calories, or replace lost electrolytes. The amount you should drink is dependent on the weather, the speed with which you are likely to finish the race and your personal hydration habits. If there are drinks stations at every mile, you may not want to stop at them all, but you should certainly be aiming for a drink every 2 to 3 miles, taking in between 150 and 250 ml – or 8 gulps – every 15 to 30 minutes.

Should you eat during the race?

Bear in mind that when you exercise, blood flow to the digestive system is greatly reduced. Anything solid you consume will take a long time to digest, and could end up causing stomach problems, as well a taking a while to boost your energy levels. If you do decide to take a snack on the run, choose something that is high in carbohydrate – particularly foods high on the glycaemic index – and easy to digest. Jelly babies or wine gums fit this category. As with sports drinks, try this first in training, to see if it works for you.

The finish line

As you turn on to the home straight of your race, with the finish line in sight for the first time, it can be a very emotional experience. It's quite common to find a sudden surge of energy that has you almost sprinting the last few yards rather than jogging. If there's a camera at the finish taking souvenir photos, ensure you look up at it, smile and don't obscure your race number with your arms. As you cross the line, stop your watch and keep moving. Don't stop suddenly, since this might make you feel dizzy or nauseous. As you make your way to the reuniting point or baggage area, use the foil

blanket, if you are given one, since your body temperature will drop quite quickly. You should find some food in your 'goody bag' – eat it sooner rather than later to help kickstart the recovery process – within 20 to 30 minutes is ideal. Soak up the atmosphere and allow your pride to show – you are a hero!

The road to recovery

The hours following the completion of a marathon are one time when stretching isn't particularly advisable, since the muscles are already likely to be inflamed and damaged. If possible, keep moving for 10 to 15 minutes after your run, as a cool-down, rather than throwing yourself onto the nearest flat surface, which will only serve to stiffen you up further. If at all feasible, try sitting in a cold bath or wading in a cold swimming pool, or even the ocean, for 10 to 15 minutes to reduce inflammation in the legs.

Sip fluid frequently from the time you stop running, but don't gulp down lots at once or you may bring it straight back up. You may be in the mood to celebrate, but try to avoid alcohol for a few hours at least, until you've started to rehydrate. Turn to page 149 for more ways to aid recovery in the days following your marathon run.

As you approach a drinks station, try to make eye contact with someone holding a drink out so that they know you are going to take it from them.

Dropping out

There are times in most people's marathons where the thought of dropping out pops into their heads. This is a tough physical and mental challenge, and you aren't necessarily going to be smiling the whole way round. If it's general fatigue rather than a specific problem that's putting you off, dig deep into your mental and physical reserves to keep going (see the 'Seeing is believing' strategies on page 90). If, however, you feel incapable of making it to the finish and believe that to try and do so would be detrimental, it is wise to live to fight another day, rather than push yourself beyond your limits, and end up ill or badly injured. It's bound to be a difficult decision to make – months of training and hard work, possibly with the added burden of sponsorship money, are inevitably big incentives to continue. Once you've taken the decision to pull out, make sure you let someone involved in the race organisation know, and seek assistance to get back to the finish area (or start). Some marathons arrange buses or trains to help runners who have had to stop, but this isn't always possible at events where there are fewer runners, and miles of open roads. This is when that money in your sock may prove invaluable.

Tips

When you're standing on the start line, don't think to yourself, 'I've got 26 miles to run' – think of the race in manageable stages. The first year I ran, I felt very nervous. I found looking back through my training diary gave me confidence, as it reassured me that I'd done all the preparation and couldn't have done any more.

– Eammon Martin
London Marathon winner in 1993
in 2 hr 10 min and 50 sec

beyond the finish line

9

⁖ Post-race survival

HOW CAN YOU SPEED UP THE RECOVERY PROCESS? HOW LONG BEFORE YOU SHOULD START RUNNING AGAIN? WHEN SHOULD YOU SET YOUR SIGHTS ON YOUR NEXT MARATHON?

It's all over – you've done it. Whether is was 26.2 miles of torture, or – hopefully – a triumphant journey that will stay with you for the rest of your life, it's important to give some thought to a proper strategy for recovery, so that normal life after a marathon can resume as quickly as possible.

During the first few days after the race you will almost certainly feel battered and sore – all those ground forces will have taken their toll on your skeleton (you'll have temporarily shrunk by 1 to 2 cm!) while the repeated muscular contractions will have caused substantial microtrauma, tiny tears and bleeding within the muscle itself, which builds up pressure and causes pain. Ask any experienced marathoner when this is at its worst, and they will tell you that two days after the race is the worst time, which is why the condition is known as delayed onset muscle soreness, or DOMS. A report in the journal *Physician and Sportsmedicine* found that gentle stretching, ice and use of anti-inflammatories all helped alleviate the symptoms of DOMS, which may last for 3 to 5 days. During this time, simple activities,

like walking or going downstairs, can cause much agony, but are a great source of amusement to observing friends and family! To aid the recovery process, take a look at the post-race survival kit, below. While general aches and pains are par for the course, anything more specific should be looked at by a sports medicine specialist, as soon as possible.

Your survival kit

Carbohydrate-rich food and drink
Don't think that refuelling ends at the finish line. A study from the Australian Institute of Sport found that high GI foods consumed in the 24 hours following a sporting event promoted glycogen storage most successfully.

Fluid
In the days following the race, continue to be vigilant about fluid intake – you should be passing urine of a pale colour frequently.

Gentle walking or swimming

Very gentle exercise with little impact will promote blood flow and help remove waste products from the muscles.

Non steroidal anti-inflammatories

Drugs that fall into this class include ibuprofen and aspirin – they will help to reduce inflammation and soreness.

Arnica

This herbal remedy has been shown to reduce bruising and inflammation and is available in chemists and health food shops.

Echinacea

Research has shown that in the first few hours after a marathon your immune system is compromised, meaning that you are likely to come down with anything that's going in the way of viruses and infections. Echinacea is a herb that has been shown to boost immunity.

Massage

Save the massage until 2 to 4 days after your race, since it is likely that your muscles will be too sore before this.

Mental recovery

One thing that is often overlooked in the post-marathon period is how you might feel psychologically. People are constantly saying, 'You must feel so proud', or 'Bet you are over the moon'. And yet, often, all you feel is a huge sense of anticlimax. It's not surprising – this race has taken over a great deal of your life for the last few months, and now it is all over, leaving one big empty space. As Cameron Burt, treasurer of Glasgow University running club, the Hare & Hounds, says: 'Once over the line the pounding and the pain may stop, but the aching exhaustion doesn't. Then the loneliness sets in, the anti-climax of finishing a marathon. The endless minutes of pain and emptiness when the crowds have disappeared, the challenge has been completed and you have no idea what to do with yourself!' To come back to earth with less of a bang, it's a great idea to have something planned in the days following the race – a few days away, a celebratory gathering or dinner, or something else pleasurable to focus on. It will be a little while before you are back to any serious running, and then, of course, you can set your sights on another race.

When can I run again?

It is advisable to lay off running for at least 3 to 4 days. Allow at least one day per hour you ran for, with absolutely no running or other exercise that heavily involves the leg muscles. The body needs this time to replace energy stores and repair tissue damage, and there is no likelihood of any fitness being lost in such a short space of time. There is no harm in trying a different form of exercise, such as swimming or cycling, towards the end of the week.

Listen to your mind and your body in terms of when it's time to start running again – for some it may be close to a fortnight before they feel recovered enough to take to the streets; others may be itching to go after 2 to 3 days. My recommendation is a week of no running, no matter how long the race took you – not only because this optimises recovery, reduces your risk of contracting a virus due to a compromised immune system, and allows minor afflictions such as blisters and chafing to heal, but also because it gives you time to re-attune to normal life, spend some time with your family and friends, and take a genuine break from running. Studies show that people who rest for a full week after the marathon actually perform better in subsequent training than those who attempt to run that week. When you do next decide to pull on the training shoes and go for a run, do not take your watch or have a particular goal in mind – simply run while it feels good and stop if it doesn't.

How long before I can race?

If you got bitten by the racing bug as a result of your marathon journey, it probably won't be long before you are itching to enter another race. But don't be too quick to sign up for anything – racing is a punishing experience for the body and you need to allow plenty of time for recovery. An oft-quoted rule of thumb is to take one day for every mile you raced before entering another race. As far as the marathon is concerned, then, that's 26 days before you next race – or, to round it up, a month. It's unlikely that you are going to have the time or the inclination to consider another marathon in the very near future, but there are lots of other races to consider. Since you've probably sampled the odd 10 km or half-marathon race in your marathon build-up, let's take a look at some of the less obvious alternatives...

> *Studies show that people who rest for a full week after the marathon actually perform better in subsequent training than those who attempt to run that week*

∴ Taking it further

ALL ABOUT ULTRA RUNNING, ADVENTURE RACING, MARATHON CLUBS...

Ultra running

When you first started your marathon training, you were probably convinced that running 26.2 miles was the extreme edge of human endeavour. Well, you might be surprised to know that there are a growing number of people out there who class themselves as 'ultra runners', and take part in races and events longer than 26.2 miles. Even 27 miles would count, but ultra marathons are most commonly 31 miles (50 km), 62 miles (100 km), or 100 miles (160 km). Ultra marathon routes often combine road and trail although some, such as the Comrades Marathon in South Africa, and the London to Brighton run, are solely on road, while others, such as the Hardy Annual, in Dorset, are trail only. Some ultra marathons are run over a set time period such as 24

or 48 hours, with runners attempting to cover the greatest possible distance in the time allotted.

For the real die-hards, there are also multi-day events, such as the gruelling Marathon des Sables, a run through the Sahara desert, during which you have to carry your own water supply, or the Himalayan 100-Mile Stage race, with the added challenge of contending with an altitude of 12,500 ft.

Now, before you write off ultra running as a sport for loonies, consider the fact that most participants do not run the whole way. They walk when the terrain or incline demands it; they stop for food and drink, or for pit stops, or even to take in the scenery. They may need to take a break to reapply sun screen, change kit or shoes, or even consult the route map. It's all par for the course when you are on the move for what amounts to a working day! There are no penalties for stopping, walking or taking a break – other than the added minutes to your finish time, but this is one kind of event in which most entrants are running purely to finish, or to test themselves, rather than to beat others.

Making the jump

You have already proved that you can complete the marathon distance. If you are considering ultra running, the two main points to bear in mind are that you will be running for longer, and at a significantly slower pace (approximately a minute slower per mile than your marathon pace). The best way to practise this is to incorporate it into your long run – so slow down and gradually increase the mileage. It might be wise to start with a 30-mile or 50 km event, so that you can run with the confidence that you only need to eek out another 4 or 5 miles over and above the marathon. Don't be afraid to include walking breaks in your long runs. Allow yourself plenty of time to prepare for the event, since you will be doing a long run only once a fortnight, in order to allow sufficient recovery time.

Get accustomed to carrying not just fluid but food or energy snacks on your runs – your body needs to refuel on the run if you are to make the distance. For information on ultra running organisations and events, see 'Further Information'.

Adventure racing

Adventure racing is a fast-growing pastime among runners who are keen to test their sporting prowess in other areas, or inject a little variety into their training. Adventure races range from extremely demanding multi-day events such as the infamously hard Raid Gauloises and Eco Challenge, to much more beginner-friendly events like the Salomon X-Adventure one-dayers, which include trail running, navigation, canoeing and mountain biking. This is fairly standard fare for an adventure race – you might also encounter kayaking, open water swimming and perhaps something like horse riding, or rope work.

One very positive aspect of adventure racing that you don't get from running is teamwork. Many races welcome – or insist upon – team entries, which not only makes the whole thing more fun but also allows each member to play upon their own strengths. See 'Further Information' for more details.

Trail events and races

Trail running is becoming ever more popular as an alternative to pounding the pavements. Trail running events are held predominantly on rural footpaths, bridlepaths and towpaths, though some go cross-country or include small stretches of road. There is no specific race length to qualify as a trail run, and, as with ultra running, you just don't get that same obsession about finish times. If you are tempted by a trail race, spend at least two training sessions a week getting accustomed to running off-road. It's also worth investing in a pair of trail shoes, if you haven't already got some (see page 38). For contact details, see 'Further Information'.

The 100 Marathon Club

Believe it or not, there are quite a few people out there who have, or are in the process of, clocking up 100 marathons. Many of these folk are members of the 100 Marathon Club, which was formed to support those runners wishing to complete such a challenge and to put them in touch with each other. 'Bear in mind that 100 Club members usually sacrifice speed for numbers,' says Roger Biggs, the 100 Club head honcho. 'We also do a lot of trail and off-road events, which cannot really be considered as races as such, although just as hard, if not harder.' See 'Further Information' for more details. Only 99 to go....

never too late 10

⁖ Running in later years

ADVICE ON HAPPY, HEALTHY RUNNING FOR OLDER RUNNERS

Our body's flexibility begins to decline in our 20s; bone density and muscle mass deteriorate by as much as 60 per cent between the ages of 30 and 80 years. Metabolism and VO_2 max also begin to slide down the slippery slope before we've hit 40. Bearing all this in mind, it's a miracle that any of us 'more mature' runners can still function, let alone run a marathon! But, of course, it is running that delays and attenuates many of these changes, not to mention safeguarding general health. As we have seen throughout this book, there are many reasons 'Why we're here,' and enhancing health and increasing longevity are among the best.

Studies show that running reduces your risk of suffering coronary heart disease, high blood pressure, diabetes and obesity. It preserves bone, keeps connective tissues healthy, and aids blood circulation and digestion. One piece of research found that six months of regular endurance exercise increased VO_2 max by 30 per cent in 60 to 70-year-olds; another found that the calf muscles of athletes still competing over the age of 60 years had an equal number and size of mitochondria as a group of 20-somethings in the same race. So age, per se, doesn't necessarily mean a slower performance.

If you are an existing runner, but new to the marathon distance, you certainly aren't alone. The number of older runners taking to the marathon has shot up in recent years. The Flora London marathon reports a 30 per cent increase in participants over 60 since 1995. In the year 2000, 185 entrants were over 70 years old. The USA Track and Field Road Running Information Center reports that 41 per cent of marathoners are over 40 years of age (50 per cent of participants in the New York marathon are 40-plus). The world record for a 79-year old marathoner is 3 hours and 49 minutes. Proof, if you needed it, that 26.2 is perfectly possible once you are in the second half of your life.

But to make your running and, in particular, your marathon training, safe and enjoyable there are a few things to bear in mind. This is particularly important if you are new to running, since you are asking a lot from your body and will need to be patient enough to allow time for adaptations to take place. If running is a new activity for you, ensure you read 'On your marks' on page 3, and see your doctor for a check-up if necessary. Also heed the following points.

Smart running past fifty

∴ Because your muscles and connective tissues are less pliable, you'll need to warm up for longer and more gently to avoid the risk of injury. Make your warm-up 10 minutes rather than five, and incorporate some gentle stretching if you still feel stiff.

∴ Never neglect a proper cool-down and post-run stretching – since flexibility is already on the wane, you need to hold on to what you've got.

∴ Don't run daily – older runners need longer to recover, especially from tough sessions; so run on alternate days, or, if you are used to exercising daily, try cross-training on an elliptical trainer or in the swimming pool (good for maintaining range of motion). You could also consider incorporating the walk-run strategy into your regime. Even Amby Burfoot, a former winner of the Boston Marathon, and editor of Runner's World in the US, confesses that he now frequently walk-runs.

∴ Allow longer to recover from hard training runs or races, and heed the signs of overtraining (see page 84).

∴ Consider incorporating a twice-weekly weight-training programme into your regime to offset age-related muscle loss, or perform the body maintenance workout (see pages 59–62) on the days you don't run.

∴ Dress appropriately. No, I don't mean that Lycra hotpants are out of bounds for over-50s, just that we are more vulnerable to the effects of extreme heat or cold as we get older – so ensure you layer well in winter, and don't overdress on warmer days.

∴ Be particularly vigilant about hydration. Research shows that older people are less sensitive to the thirst mechanism. In one study, active healthy men aged 67 to 75 were less thirsty and drank less voluntarily after being water-deprived than did younger men.

∴ As far as nutrition goes, the same basic rules apply to older runners as to everyone else. But it's very important to get sufficient calcium – post-menopausal women need 1,000 mg while men need 800 mg. This is because calcium is a key nutrient in the maintenance of bone density, which declines as we age and may increase the risk of osteoporosis, the bone-thinning disease that leads to frailty, loss of height and a high risk of fractures. Women are particularly vulnerable post menopause, as plummeting oestrogen levels can cause as much as 2 to 5 per cent bone loss per year in the five years following the cessation of periods (see below).

In general, these guidelines boil down to one thing – take it easy. There are good reasons for this advice. In a study published in the British Journal of Sports Medicine, which tracked the running behaviour of 844 runners, being over 50 was a significant injury risk factor.

Fit to the bone

One in three women over 50 will suffer an osteoporotic fracture. But what is less well known is that one in 12 men will suffer the same fate. While running itself is protective against bone loss (because stressing bone is what makes it stronger), if you have been sedentary for many years previously, you should bear in mind that you may not have an optimal amount of 'bone in the bank' to start with (the bone-building 'window' closes at around 30 years of age). If this is the case, it is imperative that you heed the advice about not doing too much, too soon, that you consume sufficient calories and calcium, and that, if you have any of the osteoporosis risk factors outlined below, you ask your doctor about a DXA bone scan. If, on the other hand, you have been regularly active throughout life, you have probably reaped the benefits of a healthy bone density.

One study found that bone density in the femur was 5 per cent higher in runners than in non-runners, and 8 per cent higher in runners than in completely sedentary folk. Improved body awareness, balance, co-ordination and strength also reduce the risk of falls in later life.

Bone shakers – risk factors for osteoporosis

> Slight build

> Family history of osteoporosis

> Regular use of corticosteroid drugs

> Smoking

> Low calcium intake

> Excessive alcohol or caffeine intake

> Low lifelong level of weight-bearing activity

> Excessive dieting or an eating disorder

> Early menopause or hysterectomy.

Heart to heart

If I had a pound for every occasion that someone has crowed 'Jim Fixx' to me, when I've mentioned I am a runner, I would be as rich as I am fit. Yes, Jim Fixx died of a heart attack while out running, but the fact remains that the biggest risk factors for both heart disease and stroke are high blood pressure, obesity, a lack of physical activity and smoking – along with a family history of these factors. Since running helps to reduce blood pressure, as well as significantly improving the ratio of good HDL cholesterol to bad LDL cholesterol and controlling body fat, you are already making all the right moves in terms of

One study found that bone density in the femur was 5 per cent higher in runners than in non-runners

157

protecting your heart, particularly if you have been active for some time. Heart health and running is one area in which you have to consider the statistics carefully. For example, a study published in the *New England Journal of Medicine* reported that the risk of heart attack during exercise is 56 times greater than during rest in inactive men, and five times greater in regularly active men, due to the additional demands for oxygen-enriched blood to be pumped from the heart. While 'five times greater' is a lot better news than '56 times greater', it's still enough to tempt you to swap your trainers for a pair of slippers. You have to bear in mind, though, that the overall risk of heart attack, at any time, is 40 per cent lower in habitually active men.

Heart health: reducing the risks

:• Always warm up and cool down – since a sudden, rather than progressive, change in the level of cardiac stress is most likely to cause problems.

:• Avoid exercising first thing in the morning when heart attack risk is higher.

:• Be extra careful in extreme cold and heat.

:• Do not exercise within two hours of a large meal, since heart attack risk is elevated during this time, as found in American research.

:• Drink tea – the flavonoids contained in green and black tea help strengthen blood vessel walls.

:• Stop immediately if you get chest pain, any pain that radiates into the left arm or up to the jaw, or severe breathlessness when running. At rest, symptoms that include an irregular pulse, breathlessness, sudden tiredness and swollen ankles should also be taken seriously, since they can precipitate a cardiac event.

Running and the menopause

Most women experience the menopause between the ages of 45 and 55 – the average age is 52 years. While it seems to be treated more as a disease than as a life stage in today's society, the menopause is simply a signal that reproductive potential is finished.

Accompanying this is a significant drop in female hormone levels – progesterone and oestrogen – and it is this that causes the symptoms of menopause: hot flushes, vaginal dryness and, most importantly, bone loss (see above). Another health benefit of oestrogen that we lose post-menopause is its protective effect on the heart. While men are far more at risk of coronary heart disease than women under the age of 50, the gap closes completely once a woman has undergone the menopause. This may sound worrying, but remember that, by running regularly, you are already less susceptible to heart disease than sedentary women, and that by continuing to be active and eating healthily you are maximising your chances of a long, healthy life.

Many women believe that running has eased them through the menopause more gently. In a survey conducted by the Melpomene Institute for women's health research in 1997, more than 75 per cent of the study participants said that running had had a positive effect on their experience of the menopause. A quarter felt that running had dampened the physical symptoms, while more than 30 per cent said it had straightened out the emotional rollercoaster.

You may also side-step one of the other, much-detested side effects of the menopause – weight gain. A University of Pittsburgh study found that of 535 women who were randomly assigned to either a diet and exercise programme or just a weigh-in, twice as many of those who did not exercise had gained an average of 5.2 lb 4 years later. Those who exercised had not gained weight.

The world marathon guide

⋮⋮ The international scene

THE LOWDOWN ON EIGHT MAJOR MARATHONS AROUND THE GLOBE, PLUS A GUIDE TO SOME OF THE QUIRKIER MARATHONS OUT THERE

Marathon running is a sport the world just can't get enough of. Globally, the number of marathon runners has grown by over 6 per cent since 2001. In addition, the number of women participating in marathons rose from 10 per cent in 1980 to 35 per cent in 1999.

While the leading marathon runners are getting faster and faster, smashing world records for the marathon distance, the average finish time is getting slower. But that doesn't mean our running ability is diminishing, just that more and more 'recreational' runners are getting involved, who don't have lofty aspirations about sub-2.45 finish times. In 1980, the average American man finished a marathon in 3 hours 32 minutes. By 1998, that time had slowed to 4 hours 15 minutes. That's good news for marathon virgins, since it means you'll be in good company, even if you're closer to the back of the pack than to the leaders.

When you first consider running a marathon, it's usually the major, world-famous races that spring to mind. The top contenders read like a tour of the world's fashion epicentres, London, New York, Paris.... The Flora London Marathon is the biggest in the world - in 2003, some 32,563 people completed the 26.2 miles. And New York wasn't far behind with 31,834 entrants.

But while London and New York are the biggest – it doesn't mean they are the only marathons worth entering. In fact, there are some great races to contemplate entering right across the globe, from Berlin to Boston, Stockholm to Snowdonia. If you are looking for something quirkier, how about the unique challenge of the Great Wall of China Marathon, or the small but perfectly formed seven-lap challenge of the Tresco Marathon, where the field is so small that spectators have a list of every runner's name?! Besides offering diverse marathon experiences, some of the lesser-known and smaller races are easier to get into, have fewer organisational hassles and may even yield a faster finishing time, thanks to less crowding.

So don't be despondent if you've been rejected by one of the biggies – there are still some great events out there, at which you can put all that training to good use. To give you food for thought, I've compiled a list of eight of the world's top marathons, as well as a few of the less obvious races you might consider. See 'Further information' for more ideas on where to look for your perfect race.

Paris

Official name?
Marathon International de Paris

When is it?
Early April.

How many people run it?
Approximately 20,000 – 14 per cent female.

What's the course like?
It's a fast course, with few undulations, that starts along the Champs Elysees, passes through the Place de la Concorde, along the banks of the River Seine and past the Eiffel Tower. A gentle descent leads you to the finish.

Why run it?
With over 150,000 spectators, it's reasonably lively, although there are a number of quieter areas towards the end. Apart from the prospect of combining it with a weekend of gastronomy and shopping, Paris is a good prospect because it's not too far from the UK to get to, and it's virtually at the same time of year as the London marathon, which means that you can take advantage of UK London Marathon training camps, races and seminars. As far as the race itself is concerned, it's known for being well organised from start to finish. Aid stations placed every 5 km offer water, raisins, oranges, bananas and sponges, and, from 25 km, lemon sports drink.

Any downsides?
It's not a good bet for slower runners, since the roads are re-opened after 4.30 hours, and you then have to battle with the French traffic. All runners need to provide a doctor's certificate, issued within the 12 months preceding the race, to be allowed to take part. Some Parisians are a little apathetic towards the race.

How can I find out more?
Visit *www.parismarathon.com* or, for package deals including race entry, travel and accommodation, contact Sports Tours on 0161 703 8161

Testimonial:
'Paris was the most beautiful city I'd ever visited, and the course the most scenic I'd ever run. There was not a dull kilometre on the route! Starting in the shadow of the Arc de Triomphe on the Champs Elysees made a picture perfect start as thousands of athletes flooded down the straight tree lined avenue through the heart of Paris.' – Cameron Burt, Hares & Hounds Running Club, Glasgow.

Boston

Official name?
Boston Athletic Association Boston Marathon

When is it?
Held annually on the third Monday in April, which is Patriots' Day, a statewide holiday in Massachusetts.

How many people run it?
About 20,000 – the strict age- and sex-related qualifying times mean they are the swifter runners.

What's the course like?
Notoriously difficult, but scenic. It is a point-to-point undulating course, unlikely to produce a personal best. Although primarily a downhill race, there are plenty of climbs in between. Most notably, the suburb of Newton hosts seven hills culminating in marathoning's most famous uphill climb, Heartbreak Hill. Though most of the hills are not particularly steep, the fact that they are later in the race makes them both physically and psychologically draining. The difficulty of the downhill sections also takes many runners by surprise, since the steep descents of the late miles torture their quads!

Why run it?
Simply put, there's something special about Boston. It's not the fastest marathon course, nor is it the most difficult, but it is arguably the most prestigious, thanks to the challenging qualifying times and the high calibre of international athletes, and it is the world's oldest annual marathon, having started in 1897. It is also renowned for great organisation. With over 500,000 enthusiastic spectators, Boston has a very special atmosphere.

Any downsides?
Challenging qualification times (for example: male age 18-34, 3hr 10min; female age 18–34, 3hr 40min) will exclude many runners. Not PB material....

How can I find out more?
Contact Sports Tours on 0161 703 8161 or visit *www.bostonmarathon.org, http://www.marathontour.com*

Berlin

Official name?
The Real Berlin International Marathon

When is it?
End of September

How many people run it?
There are more than 20,000 participants – plenty of first timers and overseas runners.

What's the course like?
It's flat and fast, boasting record-breaking times, taking you from the former East Berlin to West and finishing at the Brandenburg Gate. The course is also a bit of a sightseeing tour, showing you around some of the city's most important landmarks.

Why run it?
There's a good chance of achieving a good time, not just because of the course, but because the start area is split into eight lanes, meaning you won't take minutes crossing the start line. The race might also appeal to those with a sense of history. In 1990, some 25,000 runners took the opportunity to run through the Brandenburg Gate, just three days before German reunification took place. There is a famously lively post-race party.

Any downsides?
There is a cut-off time of five hours. Also, be aware that you are sharing the course with inline skaters, providing potential hazards.

How can I find out more?
Entry details are available from: *http://www.berlin-marathon.com*, or telephone + 49 30/30 12 88-10. For packages, contact Sports Tours on 0161 703 8161.

Chicago

Official name?
The LaSalle Bank Chicago Marathon

When is it?
Second Sunday in October

How many people run it?
For the first time in 2002 there were over 30,000 finishers. It historically attracts a strong elite field, including runners such as Paula Radcliffe, but that's not to say it's not an event for beginners, as the course and organisation make for a smooth debut. Few overseas runners.

What's the course like?

The totally flat, single-loop course is recognised as one of the world's fastest, run along broad, uncongested streets with cityscape views. It starts and finishes at Grant Park on the shores of Lake Michigan and just 10 minutes from the city centre.

Why run it?

The course is recognised at one of the world's fastest, and event organisation is slick, particularly at the start, where runners set off along the 10-lane Columbus Drive. Pacing teams are available for those aiming to finish in between three and five hours (in increments of 10 minutes). Temperatures are usually cool and pleasant. Race participants can get their family and friends to sign up to receive 'Curb Crew' emails enlightening them on how to be a good supporter before, during and after the race.

Any downsides?

An uncivilised start time of 7.30 am. Runners have six hours to complete the course, and those who have not finished will be required to use pavements adjacent to the course and to obey all traffic signals and signs. There are some parts of the course where spectators are nowhere to be seen.

How can I find out more?

Visit *www.chicagomarathon.com* or phone + (312) 904-9800 for entry details.

Testimonial:

'The last few miles are probably the least populated crowd-wise so go out slow as there's little moral support to bring you home if you are haemorrhaging. There's less costumed folk as well – there are more serious runners. So if you feel like going as part of a six-man centipede you'll probably make more of an impact than at a costume-heavy event like the London marathon.' – Shane Starling, Brighton & Hove Athletics Club, Hove.

London

Official name?
The Flora London Marathon

When is it?
Mid-April

How many people run it?
Approximately 32,000 – roughly 1/3 are women. World-class runners compete along with many club runners and 'fun runners'.

What's the course like?
Mostly flat (except a slight incline in the first quarter) and fast. It's a point-to-point course, starting on Blackheath and finishing in The Mall in central London.

Why run it?
It's the biggest mass participation sporting event in the world. There are 23 water stops, 5,500 marshalls, 440 feet of urinal troughs, 1,200 St John Ambulance staff, and 40 medical stations. London landmarks along the course include Canary Wharf, the Cutty Sark, London Eye and Tower of London. For most runners it is the spectators and entertainers around the Flora London Marathon course that help to keep them on the move – it's been described as one long street party, rivalled only by New York's marathon for atmosphere. The emphasis on raising money for charity also means it has a high proportion of people in outlandish costumes running the race.

Any downsides?
It's notoriously tough to get in

How can I find out more?
The ballot entry system opens on August 1 each year, and the closing date for entries is October for the year following. Entry forms are available from sports shops nationwide or from the Flora London Marathon Help Desk on 020 7902 0189 or *www.london-marathon.co.uk*

Testimonial:
'Every runner should 'do London' once – it's especially good for beginners as it is superbly organised, from the day you get your acceptance to the moment you cross the finish line. The atmosphere and crowd support is so good, it's almost impossible to consider walking, or dropping out.' – Neil Shires, North Devon Road Runners, Lynton.

New York

Official name?
The ING New York City Marathon

When is it?
First Sunday in November

How many people run it?
Approximately 30,000. Over half the runners are 40 years old or over. Five thousand are international runners, from a wide range of countries.

What's the course like?
It runs through the streets of New York's five culturally and ethnically diverse boroughs: Staten Island, Brooklyn, Queens, the Bronx, and Manhattan. The course starts and finishes at Central Park where entertainment, food and drink, 500 toilets and the world's longest urinal are laid on for runners. Hills, particularly in the last five miles, bridges, and turns all add to the challenge.

Why run it?
The original big city marathon, New York has become the model for others around the world. The organisation is super-efficient, despite the numbers. There are hydration and fuel stations, medical support, music, baggage handling, security, and the most enthusiastic race spectators anywhere – reputedly 2.5 million of them – creating an electric atmosphere. The mean average temperature for the time of year is a comfortable 11 degrees C.

Any downsides?
There is a long wait in the holding complex before the start of the race. There is a cut-off time of 8.5 hours, although this shouldn't deter many people. Because of its popularity, it can be quite difficult to get in. The easiest way is via a charity or tour operator.

How can I find out more?
Visit *www.nyrrc.org/nyrrc/org/home* for entry details or write to New York Road Runners Club, 9E 89th Street, New York 10128, NY, USA. Alternatively, log on to some larger charity websites such as Cancer Research or contact Sports Tours on 0161 703 8161.

Testimonial:
'No other marathon could touch NYC. No way – great organisation, unrivalled charisma, a genuine warm feeling from native New Yorkers who very much welcome you into their city. I would recommend it to anybody. Young or old, fast or slow. Simply breathtaking for the four hour trotter like me.' – Jon Thompson, Hertford.

Dublin

Official name?
Adidas Dublin Marathon

When is it?
End of October

How many people run it?
Approximately 10,000 – more than half are from overseas.

What's the course like?
The course is mostly flat and in a single lap, with the start and finish close to the city centre – but not as fast as some. The course will take you through historic Georgian streets past many of Dublin's famous landmarks.

Why run it?
Since its debut in 1980, the race has grown enormously, mirroring the 'Celtic Tiger' boom in the Irish economy and culminating with attracting major sponsor adidas. It's a welcoming race for first-timers – and not nearly so crowded as its bigger contenders. The Dublin race has been dubbed the 'Friendly Marathon' because there's a real 'craic' in the streets. It's run on a Monday morning, and an International Breakfast Run takes place the day before as a warm-up, accompanied by traditional Irish music. It's good for UK runners who want a change but don't want the hassle and expense of flying long distances abroad – or the jet lag.

Any downsides?
Water only en route (no sports drinks). Patchy crowd support, due to the Monday morning timing.

How can I find out more?
Visit *www.dublincitymarathon.ie*, phone + 353 1 623 2250 or write to adidas Dublin Marathon, PO Box 1287, Dublin 2, Ireland. For tours visit *http://www.sportstravelinternational.com/*

Stockholm

Official name?
Stockholm Marathon

When is it?
June

How many people run it?
Nearly 15,000 people enter the race – more than 7,000 are from overseas.

What's the course like?
The scenic two-lap, flattish course starts and finishes at the 1912 Olympic Stadium and runs through central Stockholm's 14 islands, alongside the pristine waters of the Baltic, past the Royal Palace, City Hall, Houses of Parliament and the Royal Opera House.

Why run it?
Considered by many to be one of the best marathons in the world, the Stockholm Marathon is ranked number one by the *Ultimate Guide to International Marathons*. Top marks were given for course beauty, race organisation and appropriateness for first-timers. The atmosphere is excellent, with hundreds of thousands of spectators offering encouragement on the way round. If the weather is hot, a few shower stalls are located along the course. A very civilized 2 pm start time.

Any downsides?
Like other Scandinavian countries, Sweden can be expensive. It can also be very hot for marathon running in June.

How can I find out more?
Visit www.marathon.se for more details, or phone + 46 (0) 8-5456 6440. Alternatively, write to: Stockholm Marathon/Tjejmelin AB Box 10023, SE-100 55 Stockholm, Sweden.

And a few of the less obvious races to consider....

Snowdonia

When? October.

Who? 1,500 contestants.

What? One of the world's most demanding and spectacular courses, undulating from 300 ft to 1,200 ft with a downhill to the finish.

Visit *www.snowdonia marathon.org.uk*

Loch Ness

When? Late September.

Who? Around 750 runners take part in the Baxters Loch Ness Marathon, which 100 Club's Roger Biggs awarded 76 per cent (second only to London in his ratings).

What? 26 miles of spectacular Scottish Highland scenery and clean air make this race a delight. Plus the all-important chance to spot Nessie.

Visit *www.lochnessmarathon.com*

Tresco

When? The same day as the London Marathon (April).

Who? Around 80 runners.

What? Seven and a half laps of the beautiful island of Tresco, one of the Isles of Scilly, positioned off Cornwall in the Atlantic. Caught in the Gulf Stream, the island boasts palm trees, cacti and white beaches. Runners must pledge to raise money for cystic fibrosis charities. Visit *www.trescomarathon.org.uk*

Great Wall of China

When? May.

Who? Around 600 take part (some in the half-marathon).

What? The terrain is both flat and hilly with 3,700 steps to conquer and some nasty hills with tricky underfoot conditions. Most of the race is not run alongside the wall. Temperatures can be very high. Visit *www.great-wall-marathon.com*

Las Vegas

When? End January/early February.

Who? Over 8,000 participants.

What? Surprisingly, one of the world's oldest marathons. Starting in the Nevada Desert, this is a fast, predominantly downhill race. If you fancy a bit of Las Vegas nightlife to balance your marathon experience, why not give it a gamble? Visit *www.lvmarathon.com*

Choosing your perfect race

- ❧ If this is your first marathon, make it easy on yourself and avoid tiny races where there will be little crowd support, extremely hilly races, and those run in extreme temperatures or at altitude.

- ❧ The bigger the field, the less likely you are to be at the back!

- ❧ Don't go for one with a tough cut-off time or you'll feel stressed all the way round.

- ❧ Have some support from friends, clubmates or family to spur you on.

- ❧ If you are combining a trip abroad with a marathon, ensure that the race comes at the start of the holiday, so you don't have it 'hanging over' you.

fund rasing for charity runners

⠿ Running for charity

THE MARATHON TASK OF RAISING MONEY TO EARN YOUR RACE PLACE

Many runners find their way to the marathon start line via a charity place. That is, a guaranteed entry to a specific race, in return for raising the required amount of money.

One benefit is obtaining access to races that are notoriously tough to get a place in, including London, New York and Paris. But perhaps even more valuable is the support package that comes with the marathon place, since it takes the organisational headache away. Your race package could simply be a fundraising pack, T-shirt with logo and a post-race party, or it could include flights and accommodation (for foreign races), regular group training sessions and post-race massage. Some charities operate a 'tier' system in which the more money you raise, the more benefits you get.

However, raising £2,000 or more can be just as challenging – and time consuming – as training for the marathon itself, and you may find it too much of a pressure, particularly if you are anxious about your ability to raise the specified amount of money, or worried about fitting in the training. If you do decide to go for a charity place, pick up a copy of Runner's World magazine, where numerous charities advertise the races they hold places for, or visit the 'charity directory' on the Runner's World website. Alternatively, contact the charity of your choice directly, to see whether they hold marathon places.

Of course, not everyone who runs for charity does so as a way of getting a much-in-demand guaranteed race entry. Many run for their chosen charity because they believe passionately in the cause, to support someone they know is in need, and/or to raise awareness about an issue they feel strongly about. You can run for any charity you like, but it is best to let them know of your intentions – most have fundraising packs, or at the very least sponsorship forms which will make your money-raising task a little easier.

Through the efforts of charity runners, the London Marathon (now called Flora London Marathon, of course) alone has raised over £187 million since the race's inception in 1981. There's no doubt about it, charities benefit greatly from runners' help. But think carefully before you take on such a challenge – the added incentive of raising money may be just the impetus you need; on the other hand, the last thing you want is to be worrying about fund raising when you need to focus on your training. For some, it may be wise to leave your charity run until you have already got a marathon under your belt and know what you are taking on.

If you intend to run for charity, read the money-spinning tips below, compiled with the assistance of the Arthritis Research Campaign, which has charity places for the Flora London Marathon, to help you maximise your fundraising potential.

Make it easy on yourself

- Run for something you believe in, not just the charity giving away the best T-shirt or race package. It will help you 'sell' your cause to others if you care about it yourself, and it will also make you feel more inclined to put in the necessary effort.

- Be an opportunist! Tell everyone you meet what you are doing and why (if, for example, you are supporting a particular charity because it's related to an illness someone close to you has suffered). You never know who might feel the same as you – from your hairdresser to the GP receptionist, to your solicitor or business colleague. Take your sponsorship form and supporting information about your chosen charity everywhere you go – you never know when you might meet someone who will sponsor you. Go through your home and work address books to see whether there are contacts you have forgotten about that you could approach.

- Be – or do – something different. Running the marathon is a fantastic feat in itself but millions have now done it, and potential sponsors may be suffering 'marathon fatigue'. If, however, you are dressing up, pledging to do something whacky on the way round, or if you set up a system in which the more feats you do, the more money they have to give, then people are more likely to take an interest.

- Get some help from friends and family. Most charities can provide you with multiple sponsorship forms so that others can help raise funds for you. If you are enlisting help from your kids, set them a 'target' to aim for, and reward them when they achieve it.

- If you work for a large company, try to get their support too, perhaps by running in branded clothing with their logo on. See whether they will match the amount you raise – some companies offer this kind of scheme. Use your company's notice board, newsletter or internal email to publicise your plans.

- Ask your chosen charity for fund raising ideas that have worked for others, and for material to support your cause, such as leaflets about what they do with the money, badges, baseball hats, stickers, etc.

- It's the oldest trick in the book! Get the first person who signs your sponsorship form to pledge a reasonable sum. Then others will feel less able to pledge £1.

- Bear in mind, though, that not everyone will be able to offer money, so be ready to suggest that they help you in another way if they can. For example, they could help you 'shake tins' outside the supermarket on a Saturday, or assist you in doing a car boot sale.

- Take the money when it's offered to you. While, officially, you should wait until you have run the race before collecting sponsorship, there will be people you may not see for a while, or who might have lost interest by the time you get around to asking them for the money they have pledged. If the worst comes to the worst, and you don't run (or complete) the race, most sponsors will still allow you to give the money to the charity.

Using the Internet to boost fund raising

Justgiving.com and bmycharity.com are innovative, charity donation websites, to which many charities – large and small – subscribe. Once you have your race entry sorted out, you can set up your own 'sponsorship web page' for free, through which donations can be made online, via credit card and from anywhere in the world, and through which you can keep your supporters informed of your training and fund raising progress. This cuts the charity's costs and ensures more of the donated money gets to the cause. It's a more professional approach than a tea-stained, dog-eared sponsorship form, and it saves the hassle of collecting money in person. See 'Further information' for details.

Organising a fund raising event

From car boot sales to a quiz night at your local pub, from a cake baking contest to a sponsored head shaving, there is no end to the possibilities when it comes to fund raising ideas. But there are a few points to bear in mind, such as what is and what is not legal, how to make the event safe and how to guarantee success.

First, think about your 'market' when you are planning what your event should be. There's no point in organising an event that your nearest and dearest won't be interested in, or one that will cost so much to put on that the net profit you make is not worth the time and effort invested. Sometimes the simplest of ideas, which are easy to set up and run, are the most effective. Come up with a list of suggestions and take a straw poll among your friends and family.

Once you have decided what to do, get planning. Choose the date, time and venue for your event carefully and ensure you have long enough to organise and publicise it. Is it convenient for the type of people you want to attend? Will it clash with a major sporting event? Would it be better on a week-day, or in school holidays?

Draw up a simple budget, including a rough idea of how much you will need to outlay (for publicity, prizes, refreshments, for example) and where the income will come from (ticket or goods sales, or donations, for example). You'll also need to enlist help to keep things running smoothly on the day, although you should be able to persuade a few friends and family members to give their help for nothing.

Stay on the right side of the law!

As far as the law is concerned, if an event is to be held in a public place, you need to inform the police and local council of what you propose to do. You may also need to consider public liability insurance, as well as facilities such as toilets, signage, first aid and refreshments. That's why the simpler events are sometimes the most effective fund raisers.

You cannot collect money for charity in a public place without a Street Collection Licence from the local authority or council. Only a limited number are issued each year, and you will need to apply at least a month before the date of your collection. A public place is any location where the public has unrestricted access at all times, and does not include train stations or shopping centres, which may be closed at night. For door-to-door money collecting (which you can do only for a registered charity), you need to apply for a House-to-House Collection Licence. This also covers collecting money at pubs. Again, contact your local authority in good time.

Finally, ensure that you include the registered charity number of your chosen charity on all your printed materials (including posters, letters and tickets) – this is a legal requirement.

Be a media darling!

You don't need to hire top writers, but it is essential that your fund raising antics and events are well publicised. Send press releases to local radio and newspapers to get some free editorial space or 'air time', including any 'human interest' angles, such as why you chose to support that particular charity, and any unusual information about yourself, such as the fact that you only took up running at 50 after a lifetime of debauchery! Local papers will sometimes do a weekly column on your progress, while a local radio station might ask you to come into the studio both before and after the race to give the story an 'ending'.

If your fund raising event is for the general public (such as an auction or pub quiz night), ensure you have maximised exposure: think about putting posters in shop windows, libraries, leisure centres and on office noticeboards; put flyers on car windscreens and get your friends to tell their friends. Send an email to everyone in your computer 'address book'.

Start your publicity campaign well in advance – you can never do too much publicity!

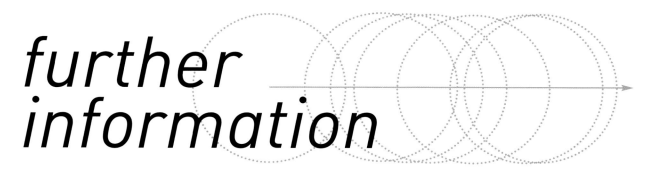

further information

Running on the web

www.realrunner.com
One of the most comprehensive running websites – with information and advice on kit, shoes, racing, training, staying motivated and more.

www.runnersworld.co.uk
The leading running magazine's vast website has everything from athletics news to race details, shoe reviews to a readers' forum.

www.serpentine.org.uk
This London-based running club's website is a useful resource wherever you live.

Running shoes

New Balance 01925 423000 *www.newbalance.co.uk*

adidas 0161 419 2500 *www.adidas.com/uk*

Reebok 0800 305050 *www.reebok.co.uk*

Nike 0800 056 1640 *www.nike.com*

ASICS 01925 241041 *www.asics.co.uk*

Saucony 023 9282 3664 *www.saucony.co.uk*

Mizuno 0118 936 2100 *www.mizunoeurope.com*

Puma 01372 360255 *www.puma.co.uk*

Brooks UK 01903 817009 *www.brooksrunning.co.uk*

Merrell www.merrellboot.com

For all shoes and kit, visit www.findastockist.com which can

lead you to your nearest specialist sports store, or email help@findastockist.com

Running kit

adidas 0161 419 2500 *www.adidas.com/uk*

New Balance 01925 423000 *www.newbalance.co.uk*

Nike 0800 056 1640 *www.nike.com*

Reebok 0800 305050 *www.reebok.co.uk*

Odlo 01250 873863 *www.odlo.com*

Helly Hansen 0115 960 8797 *www.hellyhansen.com*

Ron Hill www.ronhill.com 0161 366 5020

Lowe Alpine www.lowealpine.com 01539 740840

Socks

Hilly Clothing Company 0161 366 8207

Thorlo www.thorlo.com 0191 296 0212

1000 Mile socks www.1000mile.co.uk 01923 242233

Women's running kit

Girls Run too www.girlsruntoo.co.uk 01885 400340

Less Bounce (sports bra specialist) 08000 363840 *www.lessbounce.com*

Sports Bras UK 08700 112 012 *www.sportsbras.co.uk*

Sweaty Betty www.sweatybetty.com

Maternity workoutwear insporteur@mistral.co.uk

Gear and gadgets

Treadmills and home exercise gear, *ICON Health & Fitness* 0113 387 7122 or visit *www.nordictrack.com/uk*

Treadmills and home exercise gear, *Life Fitness* *www.lifefitness.com*

A wide range of gadgets, monitors and injury prevention equipment, *4mywayoflife* 0870 241 5471 *www.4mywayoflife.com*

Bags and bumbelts, *Salomon* 0800 389 4350 *www.salomonsports.com*

Bags and bumbelts, *Nathan Sports* 01923 242233 *www.nathansports.com*Heart rate monitors, *Polar* 01926 816177 *www.polar-uk.com*

Personal safety alarms, *MPI Marketing* 01767 652850

Speed distance monitors, *www.timex.com www.nike.com*

Liquid ice bandages, *www.liquidice.com*

Carnation anti-fungal footwipes, for stockists call 01283 540957.

Sun Protection, *www.p20.co.uk*

Anti-odour sneaker balls, for stockists call Lockwoods 01926 339388.

Energy drinks and supplements

Science in Sport 01254 246060 *www.scienceinsport.com*

www.gssi.com Gatorade's sports science institute website with information on eating, drinking, training, sports psychology, supplements... *www.highfive.co.uk* 01332 724747

Lucozade *www.lucozade.com*

Useful publications

The Rundown This guide is published annually in the UK and gives details of practically every running club, group and event. Find it in specialist running shops or order from Rundown Events, 62 Exe Vale Road, Exeter, Devon EX2 6LF

The Complete Guide to Stretching Chris Norris (A&C Black)

Nancy Clark's Sports Nutrition Cook Book Nancy Clark (Human Kinetics)

The Complete Guide to Sports Nutrition Anita Bean (A&C Black)

Anybody's Sports Medicine Book James Garrick and Peter Radetsky (Ten Speed Press)

The Art of Running Malcolm Balk and Andrew Shields (Ashgrove Press)

Pose Method of Running Dr Nicholas Romanov (PoseTech Press)

Run for Life (The Real Woman's Guide to Running) Sam Murphy (Kyle Cathie)

Running clubs and groups

The Road Runners Club This club has more than 2,000 members worldwide. For information, contact RRC Membership, Flat 4, The Woodlands, The Orchard, Belper, Derbyshire DE56 1DF. *www.RoadRunnersClub.org.uk*

Women's Running Network A growing national organisation of female-only running clubs that provide a supportive, friendly environment in which women can get into running. *www.womensrunningnetwork.co.uk* 01392 499777 for details.

National Register of Personal Trainers By searching this national database of qualified, experienced personal trainers you should be able to find one with a special interest in running. *www.nrpt.org.uk*

UK Athletics To find out details of your nearest running club, contact UK Athletics on 0121 456 5098.

Running Mates is a web-based 'running club' through which you can sign up for a real training buddy in your area or train with a virtual buddy to maintain interest and motivation. *www.runningmates.co.uk*

Cannons Health Clubs have running clubs at all their centres. Call 0870 7808182 for your nearest club or visit *www.cannons.co.uk*

The Trail Running Association is a membership organisation for trail runners and races. For membership information, write to TRA, 28 Radstock Lane, Earley, Reading, Berkshire RG6 5QL or call 0118 987 2736.

American Ultrarunning Association There isn't a UK version as yet, but visit www.americanultra.org for more info on ultra running or look at the online magazine, *www.ultra-running.com*

Injury prevention, fitness testing & gait analysis

Sports Massage Association To find an accredited sports massage practitioner, contact the SMA at PO Box 44347, London SW19 1WD Tel: 020 8545 0861. info@thesma.org or visit *www.sportsmassageassociation.org*

Society of Chiropodists and Podiatrists To find a local practitioner, call 020 7234 8620 or visit *www.feetforlife.org*

Chartered Society of Physiotherapy To find a chartered physiotherapist email physio2u@CSP.org.uk or visit the website at www.csp.org.uk metabolism. Visit *www.the-tonic.com* or call 0700 4348637

Lilleshall Sports Injury and Human Performance Centre For physiological testing, fitness assessments and biomechanical analysis. Lilleshall National Sports Centre, Newport, Shropshire TF10 9AT 01952 605828 *www.lilleshall.com*

West End Physiotherapy For gait analysis by a physiotherapist-podiatrist team and sports injury assessment and treatment. 191 Wardour Street, London W1V 3FA 020 7734 6263 *www.wephysio.co.uk*

BIMAL Medical and Sports Rehabilitation Clinic For biomechanical and gait analysis, sports injury assessment and treatment. The Hogarth Health Club, Airedale Avenue, Chiswick, London W4 2NW 020 8742 1744.

Back on Track For biomechanical analysis, core stability training, sports injury assessment and treatment and preventative physiotherapy. 64 Nelgarde Road, Catford, London SE6 4TF and Sutton Arena, Middleton Road, Sutton SM5 1SL 020 8770 4088 or visit *www.sarahconnors.com*

Exeter University Sports Biomechanics Laboratory For biomechanical and gait analysis. Visit *www.ex.ac.uk/exsport/sportbiomech.htm* or call the biomechanics laboratory on 01392 262867.

PhysioActive For sports massage, muscle balance and core stability training and physiotherapy. The Old Bank House, Mottingham Road, Mottingham, London SE9 4QZ. Tel 020 8857 6000. *www.physioactive.com*

British Chiropractic Association To find a qualified registered chiropractor in your area, visit www.chiropractic-uk.co.uk or call 0118 950 5950.

Running camps and holidays

Wildoutdoors www.wildoutdoors.info 01337 831196 running weekends based in Scotland

Runaway Tours weekend breaks in UK and Europe. *www.runaway-tours.com* 01280 840401

Jeff Galloway offers running camps across the United States, including injury prevention clinics. *www.jeffgalloway.com*

Malcolm Balk offers 'Art of Running' workshops in Canada and Europe. Email balkm@videotron.ca or visit *www.theartofrunning.com*

Sports Tours International 0161 703 8161 offers race entry and accommodation packages abroad and in the UK, training camps in Europe and the UK including at sports resorts such as Club la Santa.

2.09, Mike Gratton's company, offers training camps in Switzerland, Portugal and Lanzarote. Call 01252 373 797 or visit *www.209events.com*

TrailPlus offers marathon training camps and adventure racing weekends in the Forest of Dean. Call 01756 753803 or visit *www.trailplus.com*

Beyond Retreats running technique and yoga cross-training weekends in Derbyshire Email info@beyondretreats.co.uk, call 0207 226 4044 or visit *www.beyondretreats.co.uk*

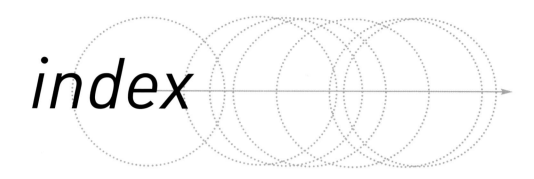

index

100 Marathon Club 153
220 - age formula 26

a

Achilles tendonitis 116
active stretching 47
Adidas Dublin Marathon 166
adidas FootScan 37
adventure racing 153, 175
alcohol 105, 107, 116, 132, 146
Alexander Technique 18
anaerobic threshold (lactate threshold) 30
animals 112
ankle sprains 117
association 89, 91
athlete's foot 119
athletics tracks 12

b

Balk, Malcolm 18
body maintenance
    problem areas 57
    workout 59–62
body mass index (BMI) 5
bone density 156–7
Boston Athletic Association Boston
  Marathon 162
braces and supports 119
breathing 20, 135

c

caffeine 103, 108, 121
calf/shin imbalance 57
    exercises to correct 60–2
calories 1, 98, 105
calculating 99–100
    in carbohydrates 94, 96
    in fat 94
    in protein 94, 96
    requirements 94, 96, 99–100
carbohydrates 96–7, 98
    calories from 94, 96
    low-carb diets 109
    see also sports drinks
carbo-loading 131
chilling out strategy 135–6
cholesterol 94, 95
cold weather safety 113–14
compartment syndrome 118
Comrades Marathon, South Africa 152
conjugated linoleic acid (CLA) 108
cooling down 46
    for over-50s 156
    post-marathon 146
core stability 19, 57, 63, 175
    exercises for 59–60
cramp 46, 104, 120
cross-training 63–7, 156
    for aerobic fitness 64
    after injury 66
    for strength 64–5

d

dehydration 101–2, 104, 120, 121
delayed onset muscle soreness (DOMS)
  149
disassociation 89, 91
dogs
    as running partners 8, 87–8
    safety issues 112
downhill running 20, 32
dropping out 147

e

Eco Challenge adventure race 153
equipment 43, 126
    on race day 140–1
    running kit 39–42, 126–7
    running shoes 34–8
    sports bras 41
    websites 173, 174
ergogenic aids 108–9
    caffeine 108
    conjugated linoleic acid (CLA) 108
    glucosamine sulphate 108–9
essential fatty acids 94–5, 108

f

fartlek 30–1
fats 94–5, 108, 109
F.I.T. (Frequency, Intensity, Time)
  principles 24